PRACTICAL CRAFTS

Seat Weaving

PRACTICAL CRAFTS

Seat Weaving

RICKY HOLDSTOCK

GUILD OF MASTER CRAFTSMAN PUBLICATIONS

First Published in 1993 by
Guild of Master Craftsman Publications Ltd,
Castle Place, 166 High Street, Lewes, East Sussex BN7 1XU

Reprinted 1994

ISBN 0 946819 46 7

This edition is a revised and condensed version of *Seat Weaving*,
published 1989 by Guild of Master Craftsman Publications Ltd.

Back cover photograph by Tony Handley.

Designed by Ian Hunt Design.

Printed and bound in Great Britain by Eyre & Spottiswoode Ltd.

ACKNOWLEDGEMENTS

I remember first with gratitude those members of my family (and one in particular) who are no longer with me but who gave me such great support and affection. In the present, I especially thank Elspeth who entered my life as a customer and subsequently became my wife; and my son Michael who as a youth encouraged me to develop my craft and whose own wife and children are fully aware of the satisfaction of creating work with their own hands.

Over the years there have been many who have shared their knowledge with me, and I am grateful to them for showing me such kindness and patience. Particular thanks go to Su and Tony Homersham; local craftsmen Jeremy Nesham, furniture maker, and Philip Faithfull, furniture restorer, and Raymond Konyn of Brasted, all three of whom have provided me with opportunities to examine many exquisite pieces made by craftsmen and to learn from them. I also thank Tony and Kate Handley, 'Country Chairmen' in Oxfordshire, whose knowledge of the harvesting, preparation and care of rushes is second to none; the staff of the Museum of Kent Rural Life, for enabling me to compare notes with Kent craftspeople engaged in a variety of traditional rural skills; and the members of the crafts centre in my own village whose separate skills leave me wide-eyed with admiration – each has added to my general knowledge and appreciation of traditional crafts.

Specifically I thank Arthur Kingdon, honorary secretary of the Tools and Trades History Society; Mrs Kong How Kooi, librarian of the Rattan Information Centre in Kuala Lumpur; Peregrine C. Sales, Commercial Counsellor at the Embassy of the Philippines in London; and the London staff of the Trade Promotion Centre of the Embassy of the Republic of Indonesia.

The photographic illustrations which accompany the text were taken by myself and have been given skilful preparation by professional photographer and part-time stick-maker Len Rooks; I am indebted to him for his advice and help.

Finally, I do not forget the help and encouragement I have received in getting this project off the ground from Elizabeth Inman and Bernard Cooper of the Guild of Master Craftsmen.

Ricky Holdstock
Hernhill, Kent
March 1989

AUTHOR'S NOTE

The objective in seat weaving is to create a pattern which is dependent upon the material used, so that the finished work is functional and aesthetically appealing. Understandably the average person is not too concerned with how the result is achieved: it is enough that it looks right and fulfils its purpose. The methods used to obtain this result are a mystery to them.

There is no difficulty in recognizing the differences between various types of woven seating. Everyone can identify a rush seat and differentiate between one woven with seagrass and another with rattan cane, even though there is no universal agreement on the names for them.

It is not always quite so easy to judge at first sight if the work has been done well. Note those last two words: 'done well', not 'done correctly', for with hand on heart I cannot assert that one method of weaving with a particular type of material is more 'correct' than another. There are no absolute right or wrong methods to achieve one's purpose in this craft. Weavers in one country do not necessarily work their patterns in the same way as those in another. It is possible for some experts to distinguish between an antique chair seat woven in the north of England with rush or cane, and one worked in the south. Indeed, not only are there regional variations in method (though these are not so marked nowadays), but many professional seat weavers have their own distinctive ways which are virtually their trademarks.

The methods described in these pages are no more 'correct' than those preferred by other workers in the craft. But they suit me. I learned the basics from my family, and over the years I have experimented with variations which have enabled me to evolve what I humbly consider to be improvements on my family's tuition.

This book is not intended to be the definitive work of reference covering every known material and method used in chair seat weaving. It is concerned with the modest aim of describing the materials and techniques required for the more common types of chair available to the majority of people – those pieces of furniture which have predominated in my workshop over a period of time and which are the most likely to be the ones that readers will wish to work on.

CONTENTS

RUSH WEAVING

THE COMMON BULRUSH

If you want to study the history of furniture in depth, you need only go to your local public library where you will find some excellent books on the subject. You may even find one or two publications specializing in the history of chairs. But if you want the history of the most important part of the chair – the seat itself – you will have to be content with the occasional crumbs of information almost casually dropped into the odd paragraph, or at best forming a small part of an appendix.

Probably because of its comparatively ephemeral nature, rush seating is a poorly documented facet of furniture in general. Upholstered seats, wooden seats, leather and cane seats all get more coverage, but the story of the humble rush seat receives scant attention.

But has it always been humble? From the large number of representations of furniture which appear on seals and other artefacts excavated at Ur (in south Iraq), it is possible to assert that rush work was known as far back as the fourth millenium BC. In ancient Egypt, too – as surviving furniture from about 3,500 years ago indicates – the

throne-chair was a symbol of honour, with seats usually made of plaited reeds (rushes?) or leather, while small stools with woven seats were predominantly used by the poorer class of Egyptian.

One wonders, however, if the material then called rush was the same plant that we use for seat weaving today. Of all natural materials known to man, rushes and reeds are mong the most ancient. Reeds have been used since prehistory to construct water craft in the Middle East. Moses' basket is said to have been made of bulrushes rendered watertight with clay and tar, but that is now accepted as a mistranslation; it was another water plant that was used, the *papyrus antiquorum.* The error was compounded in the pre-Raphaelite painting 'Moses in the Bulrushes', which depicts the waterside plants as the great reed mace and not the bulrush.

The ancient world certainly understood the value of the bulrush. Evidence for this is to be found in the play *Menaechni* by the Roman playwright Plautus (254–184BC), who wrote (Act II, scene 1, line 22): '*In scirpum nodum quaeris,'* which translates roughly as 'You are looking for a node, or nodule, in a bulrush' – i.e. you are looking for a nonexistent difficulty. The stem of the true bulrush – botanical name *Scirpus lacustris* – is leafless, smooth, with no nodes or knobs on it anywhere, and therefore ideal for twisting and plaiting. Plants which have leaves

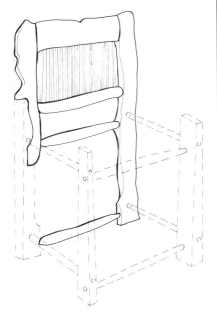

All that remains of a Viking chair excavated in southern Sweden and seen in the Kulturhistorika Museum, Lund. The broken lines show possible reconstruction. The placing of the back seat rail below the level of the side rails would perhaps indicate that the seat was woven – whether with rush or some other natural material cannot be said for certain, although the back and front rails of many old rush-seated country chairs were made lower than those at the side.

growing out from the stem cannot be used in this way, for the stems easily break at those points (the nodes) where the leaves grew.

There are indications that the Vikings wove and plaited rushes for their seating, but no positive references to suggest that rush seating was in vogue in England before the seventeenth century. However, in medieval Italy the humbler homes in country districts are known to have had simple rush-seated ladderback chairs, so it is quite possible that they were used in England during that period.

In medieval times the Low Countries and Spain also had rush seats. Spanish nobility enjoyed sitting on ladderback chairs with such seats, the woodwork often painted in rich colours. Evidence that the Dutch favoured them can be seen in paintings by artists of that country. Nicolaes Verkuje (1673–1746) in his painting 'A Tea Party' shows that by that time such chairs had gone 'up-market'.

Late seventeenth-century inventories of house property list 'Dutch matted' and 'Dutch flagg' chairs. 'Flag' suggests the strap-like leaves associated with certain plants growing in wet ground, such as the iris and great reed mace, which can be used as substitutes for rushes.

Robert Hilliand, a yeoman of Writtle in Essex, owned '5 chaires rush ones', according to an inventory of his possessions dated 1708. Other inventories of the time refer to 'an oval gateleg table and 6 rush chairs to set around it' (in a blacksmith's home, 1705); and '11 rout chaires' (*c.* 1714). A 'rout' was a common term for a large evening party, for which rout chairs were frequently hired out in large numbers to families who wished to celebrate an occasion but whose seating capacity fell short of the number of invited guests. Later, Sheraton described them as 'small painted chairs with rush bottoms'.

Ladderback chairs are of ancient design (in England they are usually associated with Yorkshire craftsmen, just as spindlebacks are reckoned to be Lancashire-inspired), but after about 1720 rush seats on them became unfashionable, giving place to the more socially acceptable upholstered seats and not reappearing until Victorian times.

The 1862 Exhibition in London reintroduced the rush seat in a most unlikely way – through the medium of a marble sculpture. 'This most admired exhibit' (it was said) was entitled 'The Reading Girl' by the Italian sculptor Pietro Magni, who featured her sitting on a rushed chair. This was a piece of furniture which had continued in use in provincial England for a very long time, but the Exhibition lifted it from the lower classes into the realms of fashionable society. A respected architect and furniture designer of the day, William Burges, gave 'the Modern Crystal Palace chair value 2/– with a rush bottom' a glowing testimonial.

Whether William Morris (1834–1896), founder of the Arts and Crafts movement, was influenced by that exhibit in any way is not recorded. Certainly, however, he realized the attractions of the spindleback chair with rush seat, which found a new market through his firm Morris, Marshall, Faulkner & Co. (est. 1861). By that date, residents of town and suburb were already yearning for 'the country life' and appreciated this return to rural values.

The ideals of William Morris have survived in English furniture to the present day, thanks to such artist–craftsmen as Ernest Gimson (1864–1919), whose simple yet elegant rush-seated ladderback chairs are still a pattern for excellence.

But who, one wonders, were the folk who through the centuries actually wove the rushes into such comfortable, attractive seats? History does not mention them. Probably somewhere in the ledgers of an old chair-making firm are the names of the employees – outworkers perhaps, with pathetic rates of pay; and some of them at least will have known how to put rush bottoms on to their employers' chairs. But to all intents and purposes they must remain anonymous craftsmen.

Dedicated chair-seat weavers of rushes (or 'bottomers' or 'matters', as they have been referred to) may be wise, but hardly wealthy, and not always healthy. Until the last century, when health authorities began to take heed of working conditions and the various Factory Acts attempted to make them a little less intolerable for so many, rush workers (particularly if they worked in their own homes at the craft) were subject to chest problems caused by the dried dust and mildew from old and badly stored rushes. 'Matters' chest', this was called. The danger still exists for those of us who weave new rush bottoms on to old chair seats, and is increased by the dirt and grime of ages which inevitably collect between the coils. One never knows what bugs and beasties might by lurking within the broken weaving, which is why it is safer to cut away old seats in the open air – never in the kitchen or the garage or the garden shed! – so that the dust can be blown away from one's lungs.

Physical aches are another occupational hazard; strange are the contortions of a rush weaver during his or her work! Traditionally such workers sat on the ground or a low stool, but it is easier to work at a bench or table top. However, you will become so engrossed in the weaving that you will not realize you have been standing and bending over the seat for too long until you try to stand erect!

In the latter part of last century rush-seat weaving was considered to be women's work, though previously it had been a man's job. Can there be any basis for the suggestion that perhaps Shakespeare's Bottom in *A Midsummer Night's Dream* was a weaver of rush seats – a bottomer – not a loom weaver?

In the past there has been a great deal of confusion over the name of the plant which we use to weave rush seats, baskets and mats. This is hardly surprising, considering how many hundreds of grasses, rushes and sedges there are in the world, which only the most expert botanist can identify at sight. To be pedantic, I suppose we should call them 'sedge seats', since the plant we use for seat weaving is a member of the sedge family, *Cyperaceae,* not the rush family, genus *Juncus.*

The correct English name for this is the common bulrush. It is a plant eminently suitable – almost uniquely so – for chair-seat weaving because its stem is as high as 10ft (3.04m) above the slow-running streams, rivers and ponds in which it grows in England. Also the stem is smooth, round and completely free of leaves, because these grow from the base of the plant below the surface of the water. The flower at the top of the tall stems is a dainty cluster of reddish-brown spikelets. The rhizomes, thick creeping underground stems from which the plant grows, were once considered to be astringent and diuretic, and were utilized in medicinal preparations. Coopers use the stems for caulking between the staves of barrels, as they have always done, but the days are past when country folk plaited, twisted and wove them into baskets, ropes, hats and footwear.

At this point, further clarification of the nomenclature and identification of the plant we use for weaving rush seats is necessary. What many folk refer to as the bulrush is not that plant; what they have in mind is the tall, graceful great reed mace, with its long brown, velvet, sausage-shaped flower growths at the top of the main stems. It is a majestic plant, with long, strap-like leaves growing like a sheath round the stem, but it is *not* a bulrush; the leaves can indeed be used for chair seating (as they are extensively in the USA where they are called 'cattails'), but they are not as easy to work with nor as hard-wearing as the stems of the common bulrush.

To add to the confusion, there is also the so-called soft rush, *Juncus effusus,* which is in fact a true member of the rush family. This prolific plant grows in dark green clumps up to 5ft (1.52m) high in badly-drained damp pastures and meadows. Sheep and cattle avoid eating the hard stems which in former times had a very useful purpose: the pith was used to make rush lights. The flowers of the soft rush grow in a small tight cluster near the top of the stem. Like *Scirpus lacustris* the stems are leafless, but their diameter is so small and their fibres so hard that the plant is quite unsuitable for chair-seat weaving. Compact or conglomerate rush, *Juncus conglomeratus,* is a similar plant. The stems of both these rushes can be used for the seats of miniature pieces of furniture despite their unsuitability for domestic chairs.

Rushes are not easily available to the few professional rush weavers in this country. Land reclamation, crop spraying, stream and ditch clearing, not to mention the vagaries of English summers in recent years, have combined to reduce considerably the number of places where once they stood.

Nevertheless, the species is widespread throughout most of the northern hemisphere as well as in parts of Australasia. In Europe it is to be found from the Black Sea to the Atlantic, in the waters of Iberia and the lakes of Scandinavia, though seldom in sufficient quantity or in accessible stretches of water to make harvesting a viable proposition. In the British Isles rushes are most commonly found in the north-west of Ireland and in those English counties to the east and south of Staffordshire. The upper reaches of the Thames and the waters of East Anglia supply most of England's rushes.

It is sad that at the time of writing there are only a handful of major rush-cutters in the United Kingdom. In summer 1988 it was discovered that up to one-third of the season's crop in one locality had been seriously damaged by pollution from adjoining land, causing a worrying deterioration in the quality and quantity of the crop.

Rushes from Holland, Spain and Portugal are imported to satisfy the British demand though many weavers consider the home-grown variety superior: they tend to be longer, stronger and to have a greater range of natural colours than their European counterparts – every shade of green, yellow and soft brown, compared with the predominantly golden and fawn shades of imported rush.

Furthermore, English rush growers allow the harvested crop to dry out naturally, whereas it is suspected by some users that overseas rushes may be dried too quickly by artificial means, giving them a tendency to brittleness.

To allow the crop to grow to full maturity, half the crop is harvested one year and half the next, usually between mid-July and the end of August – between hay harvest and corn harvest – depending on the weather conditions.

As the rushes grow under water, mechanical methods of cutting are not practicable. Instead, they are cut below the surface by rush-cutters in flat-bottomed boats or wearing thigh-length waders, using sharp blades fixed to poles in order to reach down to the stems. Once cut, they are laid out on the bank or under suitable cover to drain before being taken to be stored in a dry, airy place, out of the direct rays of the sun, and turned frequently to prevent mildew.

When they have dried out completely, which takes at least three weeks, they are tied into bundles and stacked ready for sale or use by the growers themselves. There must be a total loss of weight before storage, otherwise damp and mildew will damage the texture and the stems will be speckled.

These bundles are between 6ft (1.82m) and 8ft (2.43m) tall and about 38in (96.5cm) round the base. They have been called bolts of rush and sold as such, though nowadays they are more often sold by weight when dry; this is usually in bundles of two kilos, which is sufficient to reseat two average dining chairs after they have been trimmed and any poorer quality specimens discarded.

The rush seat-weaver's craft is one which cannot be adapted to a machine. Eye and hand working together play a major part in the transformation of the natural plant into a functional and aesthetic product. The skills are somewhat complex, but not beyond the capabilities of people considering themselves craftsmen. It is not a clean job, and not for those who like to keep their hands smooth and soft for grit and dirt from the bed of the stream or river inevitably cling to the stems while they are being prepared for weaving. However, the method of weaving rushes into a chair seat is simplicity itself, requiring nothing more than the repetition of three basic movements. It is the skill of forming the natural rushes into coils to lie compactly, evenly and at the correct angles, that needs time and patience to acquire.

Rush harvesting in the upper reaches of the Thames, near Lechlade.

Preparation For Work

A Victorian authority on furniture, Mrs Panton, urged people to consider purchasing 'the 3s. 6d rush-seated, black-framed chairs . . . which are strong and artistic in appearance. I personally' (she said) 'am very fond of these simple chairs with rush seats, if the frames are stained "Liberty Green".'

Secondhand shops and country auctions still offer such simple chairs with rush seats – not, admittedly, for as little as 3s 6d (17½p), but for a relatively small sum nevertheless. Very few will have the Liberty Green colouring once so fashionable, fewer still those originally sold 'in the white' (unstained bare wood which was kept clean by rubbing with sand). Most will be of the black-framed variety. But for the cost of the chair frame and the materials to replace the seat you can have an attractive, substantial and comfortable chair which could quite well be passed on to your grandchildren.

Not every secondhand chair is suitable for rush seating, and you cannot transform an upholstered or a caned seat into a rush one easily – if at all. A rush seat requires the seat rails to be dowelled into square or round corners of the chair legs, those in front extending a little above the level of the rails. It is possible to rush certain seats which do not have corner posts – e.g. drop-in frames and some types of stool – but for the beginner these should only be attempted after the basics of the craft have been mastered on frames which are square or rectangular with conventional corners.

Once you have ascertained that the chair or stool was originally designed to have a rush seat, go over the piece to make sure that all joints are firm. It has already been emphasized that any cleaning, stripping down, polishing and colouring of the woodwork is best done before the weaving is begun, because such work is made unnecessarily difficult once the new seat is in place.

Pay particular attention to the rails. It is best that they should be more flat than round: round rails tend to make the weaving slide along, particularly on the side rails, unless they are first roughened with a rasp.

Watch out for telltale signs of edging strips or thin strips of wood nailed to the leading edge of each rail over the rush coils, to protect the work from undue wear at the edges. These strips may have broken off; if they are still in place, as like as not they will have splintered over the years and have been re-nailed. You can replace them when the weaving is finished, if you wish. Make sure there are no rusty pieces of broken nails still sticking out from the rails; if there are, they should be removed completely if at all possible and the wood suitably treated. If they cannot be removed, they should be either hammered home or filed down level with the surface so that they do not damage the new coils of rush. New edging strips should be cut to fit over the rushes between the chair legs, slightly chamfered at the ends to fit neatly with the shape of the corners, and nailed over the rushwork into the frame so that the top of each strip (which must be smooth and slightly rounded) does not extend above the top of the corner posts of the front legs. The nails must go between the coils and not through them. Some European chairs have edging strips slotted into vertical grooves in the tops of the legs.

Rushes purchased from a supplier are not cheap, but as already indicated a bolt or bundle weighing about two kilos will be ample to re-seat two dining chairs. A proportion of the bolt will be found unsuitable for weaving: the butts (thick ends) can be too thick, the tips (thin ends) too thin, while some may be broken or discoloured. None of these rushes and pieces of rush should be discarded, however, as they can be used in the work for other purposes than the actual weaving.

Furthermore, it is unlikely that for your first few efforts you will be able to work every usable rush; you are bound to make mistakes. The technique requires much practice, and I have yet to meet a rush seat-weaver who can honestly say that he or she has produced a perfect seat. Artificial rush can be used, and the method of weaving is virtually the same (as described in the next section), but to weave a rush seat in the proper way requires the proper materials: common bulrushes.

Whether natural or artificial rush is used, only one basic pattern can be woven. This pattern is easily identified by what appear to be four triangles formed by the weaving, the apices of which meet roughly in the centre of the seat frame. With other seat-weaving materials – seating cane, Danish cord, seagrass, etc. – you can achieve innumerable designs. With rushes, the four-triangle pattern is the only traditional one.

The tools you will need are minimal: measuring tape, hammer, sharp knife or shears, small block of wood about 2in × 3in × 4in (51mm × 76mm × 102mm), some large bulldog clips, maybe some fine string, a 'rammer' (I made mine from a wooden kitchen spoon with about three-quarters of the bowl sawn off and the edge smoothed), and an upholsterer's needle or a steel rush needle (I use an ex-Army brass revolver pull-through) for easing the rushes through the weaving in the final stages when the work is tight. By the way, it matters not whether you are a right- or left-handed person; before long you will have to become ambidextrous!

Chair seats are normally wider at the front than at the back. This is only a little more difficult to work than square or rectangular seats in the initial stages, so the description of the method which follows is for shaped seat frames, including round frames and those with curved rails.

Before starting work, however, the rushes have to be prepared, and this preparation is a part of the craft which can only be learnt through experience. When the rushes are in their bolts, having been stored for some weeks or months (or even years, for if stored properly they can be used when they are a year or two old), they are dry and consequently brittle. They have to be mellowed before they can be used, or they will split and crack. Mellowing is achieved by damping until they feel as soft and as smooth as moist chamois leather. They can then be folded, twisted and pulled with little fear of breaking. They must never be soaking wet, however, for wet rushes cannot be worked well and will not dry out properly.

The length of time needed for the preparation of the rushes, and the methods employed to get them to that condition, are matters for individual experiment. There are a number of factors to be considered: the origins of the rushes (English fresh water, Dutch sea water, or whatever), the storage conditions they have enjoyed and the length of time they have been in store, and the prevailing weather conditions all play a part in deciding how to prepare them. I invariably use English freshwater rushes, and my procedure is as follows.

During the evening before I intend to start work, I select a sufficient number of the right sizes of rushes for the work I anticipate doing the following day. I lay them in the open (a grass surface is better than hard concrete, for it allows excess water to lie in the soil and air to circulate underneath) and sprinkle them thoroughly with water from a watering can. Rainwater is best, and it is better still if it is actually raining and I can let them lie out in it. A few minutes after they have been sprinkled or rained on, I turn them over and sprinkle them again, then leave for a further five minutes or so before lifting them upright and letting the excess water drain off. They are then wrapped in an old, heavy blanket which I have likewise made damp (*not* wet); the ends of the blanket are folded over so that no rushes or parts of them are exposed to the air, and they are brought under cover where they are left to mature and mellow overnight so as to be ready for use first thing next day.

While I am using them to weave, they remain in the blanket. I take out only a couple of dozen at a time from the butt end of the bundle, because once exposed to the air and with my hands continually working on them they dry out very quickly. On hot days, I sprinkle the outside of the blanket with water from time to time to reduce evaporation.

That is my method for most of the year. Rushes prepared within a month or two of harvesting do not usually require so much from the watering can, nor blanket-wrapping for so long. I leave thick rushes, particularly if they are old, in the open after sprinkling to soak for 15 minutes each side, before sprinkling them again immediately prior to wrapping and leaving for sometimes as long as 24 hours.

If, as sometimes happens, there remain some rushes unused at the end of the working day, I allow them to dry out thoroughly before damping them again several days later. To leave them wrapped for more than a day while still damp can make them sticky to the touch and unsuitable for working; they would then have to be thrown away.

Some rush weavers soak their rushes in a bath of warm water for differing periods of time – from a few minutes to an hour or more – before wrapping them in blankets, towelling or sacking. Others put the blanket roll into a plastic sleeve to prevent overnight evaporation. Whatever method you decide on, the aim must always be to produce rushes with that soft, pliable quality essential to good weaving.

A word or two on the selection of rushes. In my rush store are bundles already sorted into three sizes – fine, medium, and thick – so that I can quickly select a suitable supply for the type of chair I shall be working on. If you look at the seat rails of the chair you are planning to re-seat, you may notice some regular discolorations all the way across the rails from inside to outer edge; there may even be slight indentations. These marks show where the original rush coils were, and from them you will be able to measure the thickness of the twisted coils. You can then select your rushes accordingly.

Measure out a distance of 4in (102mm) along the rail on which the old rush marks are most distinct, and count the marks lying in that stretch. Divide by four, and you will have the average number of coils to each inch of weaving. If they average three or four coils to the inch, you should use fairly thick rushes; five or six to the inch, medium-sized ones; seven or more, fine rushes. If there are no such markings, or if they are not sufficiently distinct, a very rough guide is 'the more delicate the chair, the finer the rushes'. As this is probably the first seat you are going to rush weave, play safe and settle for the medium size. (You will of course realize that the thinner the coils, the longer the work will take.)

Your chair is on the worktop before you and you have made a space at the right of it on which to put a small supply of rushes to be worked. A sheet of plastic on which to place them is useful: they dry out quickly enough without having a porous surface beneath them to absorb even more of the moisture. Newspaper on the kitchen table is not much good, as it is absorbent too. I have made myself a V-shaped trough out of a few bits of timber and a couple of large plastic refuse bags. It is long enough to hold the rushes as they lie at the bottom of the trough close to each other, thus reducing the surface area of each and delaying evaporation of the moisture in them. I also have a small garden spray handy – the kind used on indoor plants – to mist the rushes in the trough on warm, dry days. Working in the kitchen with the central heating on full is not advised! The optimum working temperature for me is between 10° and 15°C (50° to 60°F).

Immediately before use, each rush in the trough waiting to be used must be pulled through a piece of rag to remove as much dirt from the river bed and to expel as much excess air and moisture from the stems as possible, so that they are as flat as they can be. Even while you are using them in the weaving process, compress them between your thumbs and forefingers; the flatter they are, the better the result. Wipe them first from tip to butt. The tips, having little strength in them, will break off. Hold each rush with one hand a few inches from the top and the other right at the tip, and then give a firm but not fierce tug. If the rush breaks, do the same again until no more of the tip breaks off. Any blemishes or weaknesses at the butt must also be cut off.

The method of weaving is based on square or rectangular frames. To know the shape of your square or rectangle, first measure to find the centre of the back and the front rails, and mark them. Now measure outwards from the middle of the front rail an equal distance on either side to correspond to the length of the back rail, and mark both points. As an aid during the later stages of the work, it may be useful to make equidistant marks along the back and front rails and each of the side rails about two inches apart. These marks will act as guides to show you if the weaving is straight. You are now ready to start weaving.

WEAVING A RUSH SEAT

Take two or more rushes which after twisting together will produce the right thickness of coil you have decided on. Place them butt to tip, i.e. the same number of butts as there are tips. If you are using an odd number of rushes, let there be one more butt than there are tips.

Tie this little bundle of rushes together firmly with a piece of string, the ends of which are themselves now tied midway along the left side rail. The string can be left tied to the rail, to be hidden by coils during the weaving.

Alternatively, loop the middle of a single rush round the back rail against the left corner, and use the two ends butt to tip as if they were separate rushes.

Or, knot two rushes together butt to tip and loop the butt end nearest to the knot over the left side rail about midway along it, with the knot on the inside of the frame. Twist the rushes together until they grip the side rail firmly.

These are the three methods of starting the first coil favoured by most professional seat weavers. None is more correct than the others; you can choose which you prefer.

With a shaped seat – though not with a square or rectangular one – you will have marked the length of the back rail on the front rail. If you imagine lines extended from the corners of the back rail to the corresponding marks on the front rail, you will realize that the shape thus formed is a rectangle. The sections of front rail to left and right of the two marks have to be woven first.

The way to twist two or more rushes together – whatever their thickness – in order to form a coil needs practice. Your objective is to make every coil on the finished seat appear to the naked eye to be the same thickness. While you are twisting, you will also be adding new rushes from time to time to keep the thickness constant. At the same time you will be stroking and smoothing the rushes and keeping them at the proper tension.

While the sequence of the weaving to make the pattern is simple, the manipulation of the rushes to create that pattern immaculately is not – at least, not at first. All the work is done with your fingers, and I can think of few other crafts in which one's hands are constantly in touch with the natural material: shaping it, teasing it, persuading it to take on the shape and therefore the strength that you want. It is a most satisfying way of passing one's days!

There is a fundamental sequence to making the coils: *stroke, pull,* and *twist.* The stroking is done to make sure that the rushes are as flat as they can be, and to press them together to make as it were one single flat strand. Pulling stretches them and tightens them so that the work is firm. Twisting actually forms the coil.

With your first few rushes firmly anchored on the left rail, bring them to the front rail with your right hand holding them taut over the rail. Your left hand has been stroking them and flattening them a few inches at a time. Start to twist just before you reach the front rail. Do not twist three or four times at the same place, but make the twists long and oblique by stroking and pulling simultaneously. Twist them together as they go over the front rail hard against the corner, down on the outside of the rail and back under it, twisting as you go. There is no need to twist for more than an inch or two (25mm–51mm) on the underside of the seat with each coil, but the rushes underneath must still be stroked flat and pulled tight. Twist by rotating the hand holding the rushes as if you were using a screwdriver horizontally.

Always twist every coil away from the nearest corner post and towards the centre of the rail over which the coil is being made. Turn the chair as the work progresses, so that the corner you are weaving round is in front of you. This will help you to keep a steady rhythm going, with your hands in the same position for each corner. Move the chair, not yourself; it's less tiring.

After you have coiled for an inch or so (c.25mm) under the front rail, bring the rushes up inside the frame, holding them taut with your left hand. Twist them now with your left hand but in the opposite direction (as if unscrewing a screw with your left hand). *Stroke, pull, twist* – never forget the sequence. Bend the coil at right angles over itself against the corner, but not so tightly as to pull the first coil towards the side rail. With your thumb and forefinger press the right-angled bend firmly to confirm its shape where it crosses over the first coil. Continue coiling (stroke, pull, twist) round the side rail and for an inch or two (25mm–51mm) under it, then bring it up untwisted but flat on the inside of the frame, to take it across to the opposite side rail. Start coiling again (away from the corner, with your right hand) before you take the coil over the rail, down and under it against the corner. Bring it up in the centre, making a coil to lie at right angles over the one which has just been brought across from the left rail, but twisting in the opposite direction (away from the right front corner and towards the middle of the frame) with your left hand. Press the right angle firmly in place, and bring the coil over the front rail at the corner and under it. The flattened rushes are brought up on the inside of the frame and taken towards the back of the seat, but instead of continuing the weaving, tie the rushes midway along the right rail, or clamp them to it with a bulldog clip. Ensure they are attached firmly to the right rail and won't loosen or slip. The fine string of this and subsequent ties will be hidden by the weaving. If you clamp the coil, the longer rushes can be twisted into later coils once the weaving goes over the back rail, and the clips can then be removed.

Rushes are coiled by twisting away from the corner post and laid over the front rail.

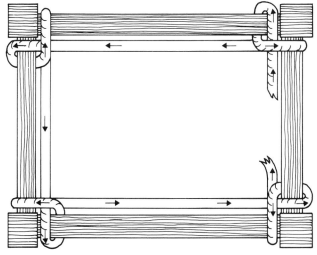

The direction of the rush coils.

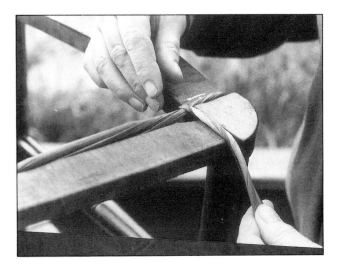

The coil is brought up in the centre, twisted away from the corner post, and laid over itself at a right angle before being brought round the left rail.

Having gone under the left rail, the coil is brought across to the right rail where it is twisted and taken round the rail.

In laying this first coil against the front two corner posts only, you have begun to fill in the extra spaces at each end of the front rail. To fill them in completely you have to add further rounds of weaving in precisely the same way as you laid the first coil. However, if you started the first coil by looping the single rush over the back rail, you cannot begin the second and subsequent coils in the same manner, as this would create an unacceptable lump at that back corner. Here is as good a place as any to describe how to join a new rush into the weaving, as you will need to do so frequently throughout the work.

Up in the centre at the front right corner, over itself at a right angle, over the front rail before being brought up in the centre and attached to the frame before the next coil is started from the left rail.

With one exception, rushes must not be joined close to the right angle crossings of the coils, since by doing so they could pull the diagonal which is being formed by these crossings out of line. Anywhere else between the rails is all right, but try not to make consecutive joins at the same point in the weaving as this could cause lumpiness in the surface of the seat. It need hardly be said that joins are never made on top of the seat; they are always made neatly with the untwisted rushes on the underside, so that they can be covered by later rushes.

One method of joining is with a reef knot, though this can create lumps and bumps beneath the surface of the seat, particularly if thick rushes are being used. In my opinion, half-hitches are better. Apart from lying flatter, with practice they can be made with one hand while the other holds the coil taut and in place. I have yet to make a reef knot satisfactorily with one hand, though that is not to say that it cannot be done. To make a half-hitch, the butt end of the new rush is placed under the old one and at right angles to it, the butt end pointing back towards the rail. The

The new rush is joined to the old by a half-hitch and both are then worked together.

Laying-in a new rush at a corner. The butt end of the new rush hangs below the frame, held in place with the right hand while the left brings the old rushes over it and all are twisted together into a coil.

butt end is then folded over the old rush between it and the new rush. Both old and new rushes are given a tight twist to hold the knot firmly.

There is one exception to the rule that joins must never be made close to the corner crossings. It is a join used by some weavers who do not sort their rushes into thicknesses before starting work but take each rush from the supply as it comes. With this method, the new rush can be added to the old at any point along its length to maintain the correct thickness. It can be wasteful, but it is quick; it is made precisely at each of the four corner crossings of the coil as the coil is brought up on the inside of the frame and is about to be laid at right angles across the previous ones. The flattened new rush is laid between the coil and the previous crossing of coils and is twisted in as

the new coil makes its crossing. The pressure at the corner holds the new rush in place; the butt length hanging down below the seat is cut off an inch or so (0.25mm) from the underside later. For this method of joining to look tidy on the underside the majority of joins must be made at the corner crossings, so that when the weaving is complete the diagonals on the underside have these continuous rows of butt ends from corners to centre. This method of joining is useful to know, for it can be used with effect to join in new lengths for the final part of the weaving known as 'the bridge'.

Continue weaving round the two front corner posts until the two marks on the front rail are reached. If the work has been done correctly the same coil will come to both marks, first on the left and then on the right.

Filling-in of the front rail ends is completed, with rushes attached to the side rails. The next coil of rush will make a full circuit of all four corners, adding as necessary any spare rushes tied to the right rail as subsequent coils are taken towards the back rail.

It is of the utmost importance to make the right angles at each corner crossing of the coils throughout the work as near perfect 90° angles as possible. By doing so you will ensure that not only are the diagonals in the weave from each corner towards the centre straight, but so too are the coils lying over the rails. There are few things more indicative of poor weaving technique than erratic diagonals – unless it is coils which are of different thicknesses.

On some chairs the creation of good right angles at the corners is made more difficult than it need be, as the posts themselves are round. To make it easier, insert a pencil-thick piece of wood vertically against the posts so that the coil can be woven against it when going round and over the previously laid coil. These pieces of wood can be removed when the shape at the corners has been established after a few rounds of weaving.

There is a limit to the number of coils which fill in the extra width of the front rail. It is not uncommon for a front rail to be as much as 4in

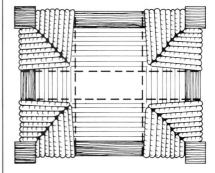

Pulling the rush coils too tightly when they cross at the corners will not give good right angles. If this error is perpetuated in the rest of the work, the coils will meet on the rails while there is still some space to be worked at the centre, which would be both unsightly and uncomfortable.

(102mm) wider than the back one, requiring 2in (51mm) of coils at each end. Using medium rushes, that would mean 10 or 12 coils at each end – hence 10 or more pairs of rushes tied to the side frames, or half-hitched to the looped rush over the back rail if you started that way. Fortunately there are alternative methods of filling those front rail spaces which utilize all four corners for weaving. For these methods, there is no point in marking off the length of the back rail along the front one.

1 As before, tie a suitable selection of prepared rushes together, butt to tip, on to the left side rail, or loop a single strong rush over the back rail. Make one complete circuit of weaving round all four corners in the way described by continuing with the rushes to the back after they have gone round the right post. They are not tied to the right side rail, but are coiled over the back rail, under it and up inside the frame, where they are coiled in the opposite direction with the left hand over the right rail

Alternative filling-in method by separating the rushes after they have come forward from the back rail to the front, and joining a new rush by half-hitch to each separated length of rush to make up the desired thickness for the coil. The right coil of the two must be attached firmly to the chair while the left one is being worked

as far as the right rail; then the second of the two is coiled and incorporates the end of the left one to continue as one coil round the back corners before being separated again as it comes forward, until the space between the coils on the front rail is equal to the space between those on the back.

A two-rush coil is separated after being brought under the back rail and towards the front. New rushes are joined to each of the two rushes by half-hitches, before being brought in turn over the front rail to be wrapped round the left rail and round the right corner.

against the corner, then taken across to the left rail, starting to coil as they approach the previous coil (again with the right hand coiling away from that corner). Then over the left rail and under it, over the coil just laid and the back rail (coiling with the left hand in the opposite direction), under the back rail. When the coil has come up inside the frame, ready to go across to the front rail for the next circuit of weaving, separate the rushes and join another rush to each of the two separate lengths. Take each of the two new coils in turn round the front two corners, tying off the first one to the right rail. When the second of the two coils has completed the right front corner, untie the first and combine the two into one. Continue weaving round the back corners, and when the coil comes up on the inside of the frame from the back left corner

and is ready to come across to the front rail, separate the rushes again and join two more new ones to each separated rush.

Should the single coil be too thick after combining the two by the right side rail, untwist it and select only those rushes which together will maintain the constant thickness. Leave the discarded ones to be either woven into the next coil passing that point, or cut off.

When this circuit of weaving round all four corners has been done, there will be two coils against each of the back corners but three against the front ones: the front rail is gradually being covered before the back one. Keep your measure handy to check the difference between the uncovered parts of back and front rails while you continue weaving in this way until the space between the coils on both rails is equal.

2 Another way of filling the front rail of a shaped seat with extra coils is to work each coil twice round the front corners and once round the back ones, until the uncovered lengths of the front and back rails are equal. Special care has to be taken if you decide to use this method, because the second of each pair of corner coils has less resistance in the making of the right angle crossing and the weaving can easily become distorted.

The third filling-in method.

3 A third method – particularly useful when there is less than 1in (25mm) to fill on each end of the front rail – is worked by taking twice the number of rushes as you plan to have coils to the inch, plus an extra two. For example: if your intention is to have four coils to the inch right through the weaving, you will need 8 + 2 rushes (10); for five coils to the inch, 10 + 2 (12); for six, 12 + 2 (14). Tie all the rushes together, half the butts to half the tips, and tie this bundle firmly to the left side rail near the back. Take any pair of rushes in the bundle, provided that one is the butt end and the other is the tip, and coil them together in the usual way, working them round the front corners only before attaching them to the right side rail.

Take a similar pair of rushes in the bundle – butt to tip – and repeat the weaving as far as the tie-off on the right rail. Continue until all but one pair of rushes have been coiled and tied to the right rail, by which time the extra spaces on the front rail will have been filled. You can then begin weaving round the front and back corners with the remaining pair. However, before you start this final pair, tie together all the rushes which have been attached to the right side rail; then tie this bundle firmly to the right side rail and cut off all the excess lengths of rushes as well as the individual string ties of the pairs of rushes.

When you have completed the filling-in of the front rail you should now have a rectangle to weave, formed by the uncovered spaces on all four rails. It's plain sailing from now on, once you have checked the right angles at each corner. Continue weaving round all four corner posts – *stroke, pull, twist* – until about a third of the front rail is covered. Check the corner angles again, as well as the distances on the rails remaining to be worked. Any discrepancies will have become apparent by this stage and can usually be adjusted without too much difficulty.

Suppose the unwoven space on the front rail is greater than that on the back? It may be only the thickness of a couple of coils. All you have to do to correct this is to add an extra coil from the left rail, round the front corners, and tie off temporarily over the back rail. These rushes can be added into the next coil round, which is started by tying to the flat rushes underneath and inside the left rail. Should the space be greater at the back than the front, simply turn the chair round and, treating the back as the front, add an extra coil around the two back corners in the same way as when making an additional coil around the two front ones.

The coils which have come over the side rails must be parallel to each other. Likewise, those which have been brought over from front to back and vice versa should line up with each other. The space in the centre of the frame must keep its rectangular shape. If the corner crossings are too tight, the right angles forming the diagonals will not be true; to correct this, the coils round the corners will have to be compressed by using the hammer and block of wood. Hold the block against the last coil and tap it towards the corner on the top of the

rail, then on the front edge, then on the underside, so that the compression is equal and the coil is straight and parallel.

When about one-third of the seat has been woven, it is time to begin firming-up the interior of the seat. Just like an ordinary upholstered chair, firm packing with suitable material helps to maintain the shape and give added comfort. The packing material for rush seats consists of discarded pieces of rush – those weak tips and useless butts you have been cutting off as you introduced new rushes into the weave, as well as any broken rushes.

Turn the chair upside down so that the underside of the seat is uppermost. You will see that by now each of the four corners has two pockets, or gussets, formed by the weaving. These pockets need to be packed firmly with unwanted bits of rush; make sure they are not wet, otherwise they could cause mildew in the seat. Use the rammer or your fingers – fingers are best: you can feel what you are doing – to press the pieces of rush into each of the eight pockets. You may need the rammer for the back pockets, as they will not be as large nor as easy to compact the packing as the front ones. Firm packing will lift the coils above the level of the frame and tighten the weave, thus making the seat more durable and comfortable. Feed as much packing into each pocket as will go comfortably without breaking any of the woven rushes.

Unless your initial rush preparation and your coiling have been done really well, so that the rushes at this stage are virtually dry, it would be advisable now to cease work on the chair for the day. As rushes dry out they shrink, and if you should finish the weaving at one go you would find that on the morrow the coils have become loose. But if you leave the work for 24 hours, when you return to it you will be able to push the coils closer to each other – not a lot, but sufficient to make a tighter weave and therefore a firmer seat. This will mean having to prepare more rushes to mellow overnight, of course.

Whenever you have to leave the work unfinished – at whatever stage this may be – tie off the ends of the coil you have been weaving to a suitable part of the frame. These ends will dry out too, of course, unless you prepare them as you do the next supply of new rushes. So damp them before tying off, and wrap a damp cloth round them so that they too will be mellow enough to be joined to the new rushes when you resume weaving. If you have to leave the work for more than a day, prepare the old ends in the way described at the same time as you prepare the new rushes.

The weaving proceeds round each of the four corners, and packing the pockets should be done after every 2in (c.52mm) or so of weaving. Packing on the side rails becomes more difficult as the space becomes smaller. While there are still a couple of inches remaining to be covered on the side rails, pack not only the

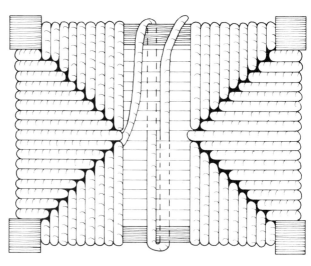

To make the bridge, the coil is taken over the rail and under the seat to come up in the centre gap between the layers of rushes. It is then taken over the top to the opposite rail to complete the figure of eight weave.

Side rails are covered fully with coils, leaving the space in the centre to be bridged.

pockets but also across the space between them to give firmness to the middle of the sides. You will not be able to add any firm packing once the rails have been covered by the coils.

Eventually there will appear to be no space left for further coils on the side rails. This is when you should rest from your labours once again, to allow the rushes to dry and to loosen. As before, when you return to the work you will be able to add at least one more coil over the side rails before continuing with the final part of the weaving.

This last section is called 'the bridge', or 'figure of eight'. It consists of the space roughly in the middle of the seat frame where the rushes which have gone underneath from

front to back come up on their way to the opposite rail. Still stroking and pulling and twisting, bring the coil over the front or back rail (depending on whether you have added a coil over one or both side rails), underneath it and up inside the frame, through the sideways gaps between the flat rushes on the underside of the seat, and over the opposite rail. Here is where you will begin to find the rush needle or upholsterer's needle (or in my case, the brass pull-through) of inestimable value in getting the rushes through that ever-decreasing space. Thread the rushes up in the centre once more, over the opposite rail, coiling as you progress but keeping them flat on the underside of the seat, and bring them up in the centre against the last coil. Continue weaving over and under and up in the centre and across until you reach the central marks on the back and front rails. Tie off the rushes temporarily while you put the last of the packing into the pockets and across the spaces at front and back.

To add rushes while the bridge is being woven, lay a new rush between the coil and the strands beneath it as the coil is being brought up in the centre. The butt of the new rush extends back under the seat in the direction from which the coil has come. Begin twisting-in the new rush underneath the seat before the central space is reached.

When the coils on one side of the bridge have reached the two central marks on the front and back rails, the

Close-up of the bridge, showing the twists going in opposite directions.

twist has to be made in the opposite direction so that it matches the direction of the twist in the remainder of the seat which has still to be woven.

If you are satisfied that you cannot get another coil between those which have been woven for the bridge, it is time to finish off. Take the rushes of the last coil, bring them under the seat and, using the rush needle, thread the flat rushes under a few of the flat strands underneath, far enough to be able to unthread the rushes from the eye of the needle. Remove the needle, bring the rushes over the flat strands and re-thread. Ease the needle under the same strands once more, remove the rushes from it, pull them tight, then tuck the loose ends out of sight.

Finally, go carefully round the underside of the seat, first cutting off to about 1in (25mm) all the ends of the rushes added while weaving the bridge, giving them a last gentle tug to make sure they will not uncoil. Trim off close to the work any thin tips which may have become exposed; longer pieces can be tucked carefully away out of sight into the rushes on the underside.

If you want to add edging strips – having cut them to shape as described earlier – place them in position over the coils along the rails. Three 1in (25mm) nails are usually sufficient for the sides and back strips: one at

Underneath the seat, the last coil is sewn round a few rushes. All loose ends are cut off or tucked away out of sight.

each end and one in the middle. For the front strip, especially if the rail is curved, it would be advisable to put two nails at each end, one above the other, and three equally spaced along the strip. Make sure that the nails go between the coils and not through them.

For seat frames which are square or rectangular, omit that part of the work requiring the filling-in of the front rail at the start. The weaving begins straight away by attaching the rushes to the frame and coiling them

The finished seat.

round all four corners to make the first circuit of coils. Thereafter the method described and its variations are the same for all straight-edged seat frames.

It can happen that, after filling in the ends of the front rail, the dimensions of the frame are such that the resulting area to be woven is in the shape of a square. In this case you will not need to weave the bridge, as the apex of each triangle will meet with the other three in the centre of the frame.

There may also be two rough-sawn rails across the back of a chair between the back uprights at a distance from each other. These will originally have been rushed. The weave for this is the same as for the bridge in the final weaving of the seat. Loop a single rush over the top rail against the left corner and coil it over the bottom rail, then take it back through the middle and over the top rail and the flat looped rush, through the middle again and over the bottom rail. Continue with this figure of eight movement across the back two rails, keeping the coils compacted against each other. To complete, do not tie off, as this would make an unsightly finish, but tuck the loose ends into the weave at the back. In joining, use a half-hitch which can be hidden by the next coil or two. Coiling over these back rails is always in the same direction. No packing is put in between the front and back coils.

DROP-IN FRAMES

Chairs and drop-in frames (loose frames which fit into the main seat frame) can cause problems if they have no corner posts to prevent the coils slipping over the ends of the rails. To overcome this a 1in (25mm) nail can be driven half-way into the underside of the drop-in frame close to each corner to act as a false post.

Secure the first coil in the normal way, then bring it over the front rail against the left end, then under the rail to loop round the nail and over itself, to come upwards against the corner of the left rail. It then goes over the coil already laid, across the frame to the right front corner where it is taken down the outside of the right rail and looped round the nail underneath as before. Bring it up the outside of the front rail and continue coiling to the rear two corners which are covered in the same way.

For the second and subsequent coils at the corners, they are taken round against the previous coil on the underside before being brought up on the outside of the rail. Weaving continues until there is no need to loop underneath and the normal method of bringing the coil up into the centre of the frame can proceed. The nails can then be hammered over the coils to hold them in place.

The first pair of coils at each corner should be placed as tightly as possible against each other. It should be ensured that each twist of the coil at the corners goes in the proper direction.

SCANDINAVIAN WEAVE

Where the side rails of a seat frame are as long as or longer than the front rail, to follow the method described would mean that the front and back rails – not the side ones – would be filled first; this would leave the bridge to be woven from side to side, which would make the seat not too comfortable to sit on.

To get round this problem, the method of initial coiling round the front corner posts is adapted to ensure that the side rails, not merely the front one, are also filled sufficiently before the weaving round all four posts can be started. This method can also be used on a normal shaped chair to make an attractive variation on the basic pattern.

Two or more rushes which when coiled will produce the thickness you aim to achieve are tied firmly together, butt to tip, and on to the left end of the front rail as near to the left corner as possible, with the weaving ends pointing to the right. Start to coil an inch or two (51mm–102mm) before going over the right side rail

against the corner. Bring the coil underneath the rail, up inside the frame, and back untwisted to the left side rail. Start to coil again with your left hand, in the direction away from the front left corner post, just before you reach the left rail. Coil over the rail, underneath it and up and across again to the right rail. Continue with this coiling over both side rails until

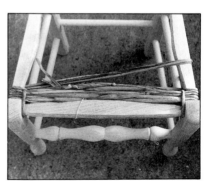

With the Scandinavian weave, the work is started by tying rushes to the front rail and coiling them four times over both side rails before the coil is brought up in the centre and over the four coils and front rail at a right angle. The number of long wraps over both side rails is reduced to three, then two, as necessary until the side rails are fully covered.

there are four coils laid over the right rail.

The coil is now brought up on the inside of the frame, forward over the four coils and over the front rail against the corner, twisting away from the corner and towards the centre of the frame. (The direction of the twist at each corner is as for the basic method.) Be very careful when making this first corner crossing that you do not pull the four coils laid from side to side out of shape: the right angles here must be accurate.

Now bring the coil under the front rail, then back up on the inside of the frame to make a wrap over the right rail against the four coils. Bring the rushes up and across to the left rail to make a fourth coil on that side, then round the rail, up on the inside and forward to cross over the four coils and the front rail against the corner, making a good right angle as you cross. Continue round over the front rail and up on the inside, then back over the side rail against the four coils to make a wrap before taking it across to the right side rail again. This sequence is repeated three times more before reducing the number of coils going across from rail to rail to three, for three circuits of the two front posts; then to two, until the distance still to be woven over the front rail equals the length of the back rail. Weaving then continues as for a normal seat, packing and checking the angles and parallels from time to time.

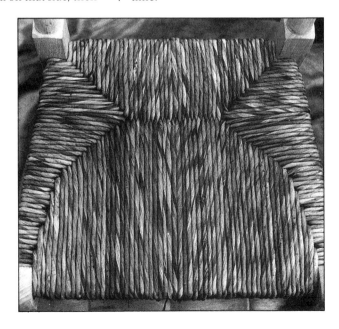

The finished seat.

First circuit of coiling on a round frame. Note the notches in the rail edges; it is also useful to notch rails which are smooth and round. Note also the insertion of four pieces of dowelling or pencil against the round posts to help make good right angles.

FIBRE RUSH

The advantage of using fibre rush instead of natural rush on a seat is that you can create the same pattern with much less effort and know-how. A true craftsman will never use fibre rush if natural rush is available, but for a beginner it can be quicker and less costly.

Fibre, or artificial rush, is made of two shades of paper machine-twisted into coils, and is sold in coils of about 300ft (91.4m); one coil should be enough to weave an average chair seat. It must never be dampened before use.

Cut off about 30ft (9.14m) from the coil; anything longer would tend to twist as you weave, and you would spend as much time unravelling as weaving. You may find that winding it into a ball or on to a reel is easier. If it feels extremely dry, it is permissible to pull it through a damp cloth as you work – *not* a wet one.

Make a simple knot at one end and tack or nail through it on to the inside of the left rail. Take the coil over the

The end of the fibre rush is attached to the left rail by nailing through a knot. It is then worked round each corner in the same direction as the weaving of a natural rush seat.

front rail against the left corner post, under the rail, up on the inside of the frame, then back over itself and over the left rail against the corner. Bring it up on the inside of the frame and across to the right rail, over that rail and up in the centre. Take it over itself at a right angle against the corner, round and under the front rail, and out towards the back.

Whether you are working on a shaped, square or rectangular seat, the weaving sequence is precisely the same as for natural rush. The advantage is that you will not have to twist and add new rushes as you work: just maintain the tension and ensure that the crossings at the corners are at 90° from start to finish.

After weaving 1in (25mm) or so, hold the block of wood against the last woven coil and tap it firmly against its neighbour to keep the weave straight and to help the formation of good right angles. Do this at every inch or thereabouts of weaving.

To make the seat more comfortable and firm, it must be packed. With natural rush seats, natural rushes are used for packing. With fibre rush, there are different methods of doing it.

When you have woven about three-quarters of the way across the front rail, turn the chair upside down so that you can work at the packing more easily. The eight corner pockets which have been formed (two at each corner) can be packed with brown paper, but this tends to rise up between the individual coils on the top of the seat and separate them. The recommended method is to prepare triangles of corrugated cardboard.

These triangles should have their bases long enough to fit against each rail between the layers of weaving after being tucked into the two pockets at either end. The apex of the first triangle must be at the centre of the seat, and each succeeding triangle slightly smaller. Pack as many of these triangles against each rail and

Packing with corrugated cardboard triangles between the layers of weaving, both above and below the seat.

into the weaving as will comfortably fit, to tighten the bottom of the seat. Then cut off the top of each triangle at the apex so they appear to have been layered. Turn the chair up the right way and carry out the same procedure on the top of the seat between the top coils and the weaving beneath.

An alternative packing method is to insert two identical shapes of corrugated cardboard against each rail, one on the underside and one on the top of the seat, and to pack between them with screwed-up pieces of brown paper until the same tightening effect has been achieved.

Continue weaving with the natural rush technique until all four sides of the frame have been covered. If a bridge has to be formed, use a steel rush needle or upholsterer's needle to weave the coils. To finish, tack the last fibre rush end to the underside of the rail it has come round, then cut it off

leaving about 4in (102mm) to be tucked away between the weaving on the underside. Finally, if the coils are uneven on the top of the seat, tap them flat with the wood block and hammer, or roll over them with a round piece of wood.

Some people recommend that the surface of the fibre rush, top and underneath the seat, should be sealed with shellac, or colour or clear varnish. I suppose that would make it somewhat easier to keep clean, but I prefer to leave it as it is.

Weaving with fibre rush is good practice, particularly on square or rectangular seat frames such as stools, and the material is quite good enough to make a presentable seat for a modest piece of furniture. However for chairs of high quality, particularly if antique, only natural rush is really acceptable. When our antique chairs were made, the makers had never heard of artificial rush anyway.

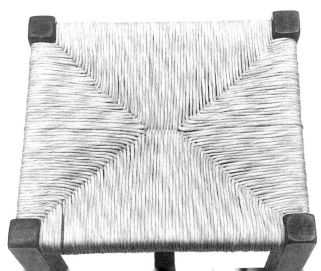

The finished seat.

2
SEAGRASS AND CORD

WEAVING WITH OTHER MATERIALS

Many of the following methods and patterns can be very easily adapted for different materials, e.g. the check pattern in seagrass can be woven in other cords such as Danish cord, whipcord, polycord or even string. One of my farming friends has woven this pattern all over the metal frame of a garden lounge chair with considerable success, using the ubiquitous binder twine.

There are so many different manufactured materials available which can be used for seating that it would be impossible to give examples of every variation, so I shall describe those which I have found to be the most popular. Once you have got the hang of it, there is no reason why you should not experiment with other materials and design your own patterns.

These materials, mostly man-made, provide a quick and attractive way of introducing beginners of all ages to the more demanding disciplines of natural materials such as rushes and seating cane. Stool frames – for which the majority of the materials in this section are best suited – can be purchased for a few pounds from most handicraft suppliers, assembled or unassembled.

SEAGRASS

Seagrass is manufactured in China and elsewhere in the Far East by the twisting of sedge or coarse grass mechanically into long continuous cords. The thickness can vary, and it is available in the natural shade or dyed to a variety of other colours. It is sold in hanks usually of half a kilo weight. 1½ hanks are enough for a stool 12in × 12in (30.5cm × 30.5cm).

Rather stiff and coarse to work with, it is best used for three basic patterns and is not suited to the more intricate designs. The tools you will need are a small hammer, a few tacks or small nails, two steel seagrass needles (one short, one long), and two tension sticks long enough to lie across the frame. The thickness of these tension sticks will depend on the tension created in whichever pattern you choose. A wooden reel on which to wind the long cords may be useful, or they can be wound into balls to prevent them from getting tangled and knotted during the first stage of the work.

RUSH PATTERN

Seagrass has been used for many decades as a cheap substitute for natural rushes. Its main disadvantages are that it is the least supple of materials to work, and it is rough on the hands. However, for a quick and cheap way of weaving a stool seat it is more than adequate.

I shall not go into detail with the method, since it is exactly the same as that for natural rush – except, of course, that you do not have to twist and add new rushes. However, there are several points worth noting.

It is not as easy as with the natural rush method to keep the work tight, particularly when making the corner crossings. Long cords going from one rail to the opposite side tend to ride up over each other, so they will need to be pulled very tight.

On the other hand, joins will be few and far between on the underside of the seat, made either with a tight reef knot or by splicing the new end with the old one. To make this splice, separate the individual strands in the seagrass about 4in (102mm) from the ends of each piece, and thread each end between the separated strands of the other. To make quite sure they do not pull apart, separate the strands again slightly further along so that the two ends can be spliced into their opposite lengths once more. Then pull the cord tight so as to make the join as flat as possible.

A variation on the rush pattern is designed to give a better finish to the work, but you will need to take a little more care in the weaving. The method, which can only be properly woven on a square or rectangular frame, uses double strands.

Start by knotting the end of the seagrass and nailing through the knot on to the inside of the left side rail against the corner. Bring it over that rail, then up on the inside of the frame and take it across to the right side rail. Lay it over the rail and bring it back across to the left rail; over and

Two lengths of seagrass have been spliced. The long ends must now be pulled very tight to secure the join.

The first double circuit.

under the left rail, and back across to the right rail. Bring it up on the inside of the frame, over the two coils and the front rail to make a crossing, then take it underneath towards the back; over and round the back rail, and back to the front; round the front rail and across to the back again. Take it round the back rail, up inside the frame, and over the coils and the right rail against the corner.

Take it over and under the right rail, then across to the left rail where it goes over against the corner, round and up on the inside and back to the right rail; over and under the right rail and back to the left, where it goes over the rail and up on the inside. Then over the coils and the back rail against the corner before being brought over to the front rail, round it and across to the back rail, returning to the front rail, where the second circuit begins.

You will notice that the weaving consists of two coils instead of single ones, and the sequence is the same across the frame. However, if you need to make a bridge after the two sides have been completely filled in, this is woven with single coils, not double. The double crossings at each corner are to help the coils to lie flat and straight.

The finished seat.

CHECK PATTERN

This is just about the simplest of all weaving patterns, yet very attractive, and it can be made even more so by laying the warps in one colour and the weft in another. It is woven on a rectangular or square frame. Although this description of the method is based on a four-coil weave, further variations can be achieved by using a different number of coils – three or five are the most common, with only one short wrap between each block.

To assist in keeping the work straight, make a guide mark in the middle of each rail. If you think about it, the warp strands of a weaving loom are longer than the weft, so you will regard one of the short rails of a rectangular seat frame as the front rail, the longer rails being the side rails.

Place the two tension sticks in position at the marks on the side rails, one across the top of the frame and the other on the underside. To hold up the lower stick, tie it at both ends to the top one.

Tie a knot in the end of a length of seagrass and nail it to the inside of the front rail against the corner post on the left. To lay the warp, bring the cord up and over the front rail against the corner, and once again, to make two short wraps round the front rail. Try to enclose the knotted end beneath the wraps to hold it secure. Then take the cord beneath the frame and the tension stick to the back rail where, bringing it up on the outside of the rail, you make two short wraps against the corner. Bring it out and over the back rail and across to the front (over the top tension stick); then take it under and over the two rails and the tension sticks three more times, so that there will be four coils lying side by side across the seat, with two wraps at the corners of both rails. On the underside of the seat the first of the four coils will be separated at the back by the two short wraps. This is of no consequence; it will happen with every block of four coils.

Repeat this sequence of two short wraps followed by four long ones across the frame from front to back until the warp has been fully laid. As you work keep pushing the cords together, making sure – by measurement, using the middle marks and the corner posts – that they are lying straight and parallel. The warp cord will finish at the back right corner after two short wraps round the back rail. Compress the cords together on the rails or ease them apart, so that the middle guide marks lie between the two cords which are at the exact centre of the warp. It is better to compress rather than to ease apart, so as to get the tightest possible warp, but if they do have to be eased apart to get the same

The first set of four warp cords is in place and the cord goes underneath to the back rail to make two short wraps before starting the second set of four warp cords.

number of coils on either side of the central marks, it must be for not more than the width of a single coil. If need be, compress the cords together during the work by tapping the block against them with the hammer.

By now you will have had to unwind the seagrass from the ball or reel because there is not enough space between the frame and the warp to pass it between them.

For the weft, bring the seagrass round the corner post and down the outside of the right rail against the corner. Make a double wrap round this rail, then insert the weaving end into the eye of the seagrass or other needle so that you can weave more easily. Weave the underside of the seat first, under and over each block of four warp cords across to the left rail. Make two short wraps round this rail, then weave the top of the seat in blocks of four back to the right rail, before weaving back on the underside. Repeat this weave – under and over each block of four warp cords beneath and on top of the frame – three more times. Then make two short wraps on the right rail, and weave back underneath the seat to the left rail in reverse sequence – e.g.

over where you went under, and under where you went over, in blocks of four cords – and make two short wraps round the left rail. Then weave on the top of the seat back to the right rail, also in reverse order of the first blocks of four cords. After you have woven one or two of these blocks of four cords with double short wraps round the rails between each block, remove the tension sticks as by this time the weft will be taking up the tension of the warp.

Continue with this weaving sequence until the weft is completed, pushing the cords tightly against each other and keeping them straight and parallel. Finish with a double wrap at the front end of each side rail, then nail the cord to the frame close to the final wrap and weave a few inches into the weaving on the underside. Check that there are the same number of weft cords on each side of the middle marks on the side rails, so that the pattern is equally balanced.

Sufficient tension has been created in the weaving to permit the tension sticks to be removed. Because the tension increases as the work progresses, a short seagrass needle can help to get the seagrass between each block.

The finished seat.

When you are weaving on the underside you will notice that the blocks of four cords do not all lie parallel, the end one being on a diagonal line and separated from the other three at one end by the two short wraps. This is immaterial: weave under and over four strands at a time as on the top of the work.

CHEVRON PATTERN

This pattern, which like the previous one works only on rectangular or square frames, can also be made more attractive by the use of two contrasting colours of seagrass – or more, if you wish to plan ahead to make blocks or streaks of different shades. Naturally, you will have to make more joins if you are going to use three or more colours.

Once again, treat one of the short rails as the front and lay the warp lengthways between front and back with the longest cords. You do not need to make middle marks on the rails for this pattern, nor do you require the tension sticks.

The warp is made by first making one short wrap over the front rail against the left corner, where the end of the cord has been attached by a nail through a knotted end. The cord is then taken under the frame to the back for a short wrap against the back left corner, then over to the front rail and under it, and round it to make another short wrap. Then over it goes to the back rail again for another short wrap between the two warp cords before being brought back underneath to the front. The warp consists only of these alternate short and long wraps over the frame, finishing with a short wrap round the back rail against the right corner. Bring the cord down by the corner post between the frame and the last warp cord. When laying the warp, pull each long cord firmly, but not over-tight, across the frame with equal tension.

To weave the pattern into the warp, it would be easier to turn the seat round so that the corner where the warp finished becomes the bottom left corner from where the weaving starts. You will need to thread the seagrass into the eye of the long seagrass needle.

The pattern is repeated as many times as necessary to fill the frame, and consists of 15 rows of cord lying against each other over the two side (long) rails without short wraps. The second half of each pattern is in reverse sequence to the first.

Having brought the seagrass out under the left side rail, thread the needle over three cords and under three cords across the seat. That is *Row 1.* Do not worry if there are fewer than three cords to weave when you reach the right rail; that will be sorted out by the pattern, as you will see when you weave the next row. Bring the cord back under the seat to the left rail. It is not necessary to weave

The warp.

the underside of the seat, because without tension sticks the tension in the warp will be increased sufficiently to keep the weaving taut.

For *Row 2,* weave over two cords by the left rail; then under three and over three all the way across to the opposite rail. Bring the cord back under the seat.

For *Row 3,* weave over one coil first; then under and over three at a time.

Row 4 – under three, over three, all the way across.

Row 5 – under two; then over and under three across to the right rail.

Row 6 – under one; then over and under three, and so on.

Row 7 – over three, under three, across to the right rail.

Row 8 – over two; then under and over three alternately to the right rail.

This is the middle row of the pattern. From here on, the sequence is woven in reverse:

The first complete pattern. The sequence so far is repeated right across the seat.

Row 9 – as row 7 (over three, under three).

Row 10 – as row 6.

Row 11 – as row 5.

Row 12 – as row 4.

Row 13 – as row 3.

Row 14 – as row 2.

Row 15 – as row 1.

That completes the first full pattern. Continue weaving the second repeat pattern:

Row 16 – as row 2.

Row 17 – as row 3.

Row 18 – as row 4, and so on.

To finish, tie the end of the cord onto a warp cord underneath, and tension it by nailing to a convenient part on the inside of the frame close to the corner.

You can vary the pattern by making the weaving pattern only 13 rows in depth, reversing the weaving sequence after *Row 7;* or you can make it a 17- or 19-row pattern. To obtain good chevrons, it is best to weave an odd number of rows.

This method means that the sides of the pattern are unlikely to be identical. It does not detract from the general appearance, but if you are a stickler for precision you can count the number of warp cords, find the middle one, and count outwards in blocks of three to the sides, adjusting the first row of weaving so that one, two or three cords are woven over first by the left side rail.

The finished seat.

CORD

As explained previously, it would not be possible to describe every pattern and variation using the many different kinds of man-made materials; the permutations seem to be endless. Any suitable material can be utilized for this sample pattern, which uses two colours of polycord. Polycord is corded polythene and is sold in spools. Two spools of red and maize were used for the 12in × 12in (30.5cm × 30.5cm) stool illustrated, and there is a lot of cord remaining.

There is no need to make joins using the following method. No short warps between the warp cords are required, but both tension sticks are needed.

The warp cord is attached to the side rail by a nail, and is wound over and under the frame and tension sticks; for a rectangular frame, the sticks would be laid over the shorter rails to lay a long warp which would make the weaving easier. The warp cords lie against each other across the frame.

For this pattern, on a frame with these dimensions I laid 79 warp cords from the maize-coloured spool and 76 weft cords from the red one, having first worked the design on a sheet of graph paper. The weft consists of 19 blocks with four cords in each. The tension sticks can be removed after a few blocks of weaving, when the tension has been established.

Thread the weft cord through the eye of a long weaving needle. For the first row, weave under 12 warp cords, over 8, under 39, over 8, and under 12; then back beneath the seat in the same sequence. Weave another three cords in the same sequence on both surfaces of the seat, to form the first block of four cords (*Block 1*).

Block 2 – weave over 4, under 12, over

8, under 31, over 8, under 12, over 4. Weave the same underneath. Do this three more times to make the second block of four cords.

Block 3 – over 8, under 12, over 8, under 23, over 8, under 12, over 8; and back underneath.

Block 4 – under 4, over 8, under 12, over 8, under 15, over 8, under 12, over 8, under 4; back underneath.

Block 5 – under 8, over 8, under 12, over 8, under 7, over 8, under 12, over 8, under 8; back underneath.

Block 6 – under 12, over 8, under 12, over 15, under 12, over 8, under 12; back underneath.

Block 7 – over 4, under 12, over 8, under 12, over 7, under 12, over 8, under 12, over 4; back underneath.

Block 8 – over 8, under 12, over 8, under 23, over 8, under 12, over 8; back underneath.

Block 9 – under 4, over 8, under 12, over 8, under 15, over 8, under 12,

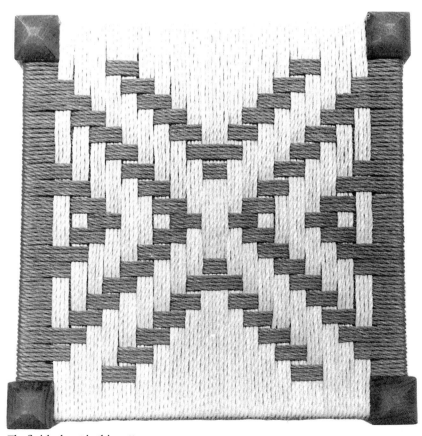

The finished seat in this pattern.

over 8, under 4; back underneath.
Block 10 – under 8, over 8, under 12, over 8, under 7, over 8, under 12, over 8, under 8. This block is the middle one of the pattern.

The two middle strands of Block 10 should lie in the middle of the side rails. The weaving sequence is now reversed:

Block 11 – as block 9 (under 4, over 8, under 12, over 8, under 15, over 8, under 12, over 8, under 4).
Block 12 – as block 8.
Block 13 – as block 7.
Block 14 – as block 6.
Block 15 – as block 5.
Block 16 – as block 4.
Block 17 – as block 3.
Block 18 – as block 2.
Block 19 – as block 1.

Finish by nailing the final cord into the inside of the rail and weaving a few inches of the end into the weave underneath.

Whenever you wish to weave a pattern with two halves identical (in other words, when you reverse the weaving sequence halfway through), it is often an advantage to start weaving from the centre of the frame. This will ensure that the pattern finishes at the same point at each end. It is always better to map out the pattern on squared paper first; a school exercise book ruled with squares for sums is ideal.

First, count the warp cords to ascertain the middle one, and also mark the side rails in the middle. It is a good idea to tie a piece of cotton or wool to each end of the middle cord, so that if you should have to refer to it again you will not need to count them all.

The exact centre of the pattern will be at the point where an imaginary line from the two marks on the side rails crosses the middle strand. From there, by reference to your plan, you will be able to count outwards to find where the middle of the pattern comes on the rails. Then, by counting the cords down to a corner, you can work out at which point of the pattern the weaving must start. If you have done your sums correctly, both sides of the first row (and therefore the first block) will be identical.

Alternatively, having worked out where the middle of the pattern is, instead of counting the warp cords to the corner you can start weaving one half of the pattern first, from the middle out to the sides. When one half of the pattern has been worked – and while weaving, do be sure not to push the middle weft cord over into the other half, or the pattern will not match – use a reef knot to tie another length of cord to the end of the first cord which you have left in the middle and weave the second half of the pattern. Finish off both ends as already described.

DANISH CORD

Made in Denmark and used mainly but not exclusively for chairs made by the firm of Møllers and others, the manufacturers of the material describe it as 'paper twine, unlaced, 3/400, in balls of approx. 5 kilos'. The 5 kilos consist of 2050ft (625m) of this heavy-duty cord, which is also obtainable in hanks of about one kilo – sufficient for a single chair. It is not suitable as a substitute for natural or fibre rush because of its tight twist, but it can be used for some of the simpler weaving patterns on stools. However, its primary purpose is for the seats of these easily identified contemporary dining chairs.

During the German occupation of Denmark during the 1939–45 war, when vehicle tyres were impossible to obtain, the manufacturers of this paper twine produced a cord which could be used in place of tyres; this goes to show how hard-wearing this particular paper product can be! I do not know what happened to the vehicles when it rained, but assume that one would not dream of damping the paper twine before starting to weave with it. Unravel each end, and you can clearly see that it is made of strips of brown paper twisted to give a smooth and consistent surface area.

Strictly speaking, Danish cord-seated chairs are identifiable, not only

by the depth of the rails but more especially by the weaving method employed, which is by looping the cord round special L-shaped nails on the inside of the rails. However, not all such chairs are woven by this means, and an alternative method will be described.

The L-shaped nails can be purchased in this country, but if you experience difficulty in getting them, short 1in (25mm) wire nails with small heads can be used instead; you will require about 130. You will also need a hammer, sharp knife or sturdy scissors (it may be twisted paper, but it is tough to cut), an old screwdriver with the blade edge made smooth, a pair of long-nose pliers for grasping the end of the cord in difficult places, and about 450ft (136.8m) of Danish cord for each chair.

If you are preparing to re-weave a seat which still has the old one *in situ*, be thankful: you will be able to count the number of warp pairs of cord and the number of wraps between them on the front and back rails. And there the L-shaped nails will be, already in place on the inside of each rail. Having studied the old seat and the way it was woven, you can now remove it; cut away the seat close to the inside of the frame, then loosen (but do not remove) the nails just enough to allow the loops of cord to be lifted from them. On some Danish-type chairs of this design you will find that the loops on the inside of the rails have been held in place by stapling. Every one of these scores of staples must be removed, even those which are clustered together on the corner posts. This was the case with the chair illustrated.

If you have a chair which has not had the seat woven by looping round nails, you have to put them in yourself. Start with the back and front rails – usually there are 19 nails in each. Measure one-third of the depth of each rail from the top on the inside, and mark a line from corner to corner. On these chairs the side rails are level but the front and back ones invariably slightly saddle-shaped, so keep these two lines you draw on the inside of the frame parallel to the top. At each corner of both rails put two nails, the first below and the second above the line, and about ⅜in(10mm) apart. Fifteen more nails

The starting end of the cord is looped over the first nail in the front rail against the left corner.

should be nailed into the sides of both rails, at equal distances along the guide line. Do not knock any nail into a rail for less than half its length. With L-shaped nails, nail them so that the foot of the 'L' is pointing upwards and leave space between the foot and the rail for a cord to be hooked over it. If using ordinary nails, knock them in at a slight angle upwards so that when the warp and the weft have been laid they can be bent over the cords looping round them, to form hooks.

Now turn to the side rails. On a normal dining chair of this design there will be at least 46 pairs of weft cords, requiring one nail for each pair on the inside edge of each side rail. Draw two lines from back corner to front on both rails – the top line one-third of the distance from the top, the lower line two-thirds. Make 23 marks equally spaced on the upper line (one end being ⅛in (3mm) from the back end of the rail) and 23 on the lower one, staggered so that the nails on the lower row are midway between those on the upper.

The chair is now ready to receive its new woven seat.

In this method, the pairs of warp cords are laid first and the wraps between them added separately. You will not need to cut off any predetermined length of cord, or to coil it into a ball or on to a reel; it can be used straight from the spool or hank. Using it in this way – one

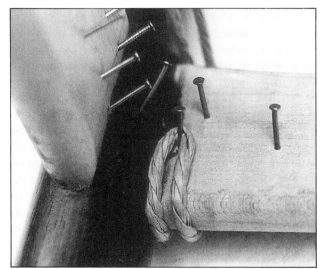

The cord comes over the top of the seat frame, down the outside of the back rail, and up on the inside to be looped over the first nail, before returning up the outside of that rail and back across the top of the frame to the front.

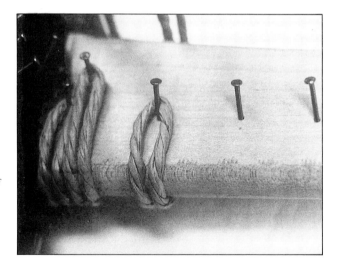

After three pairs of warp strands have been worked, the loops at the back should look like this.

continuous length for the warp and another for the weft – there will be no need for joins.

Bring an end up inside the frame and loop it round the first nail on the inside front rail on the left, with the end pointing to the middle of the front rail. The cord is then brought down over its end, under the rail to the outside, up over the top and across to the back, then underneath the back rail to be looped round the first nail at the corner. It is then brought down underneath the rail,

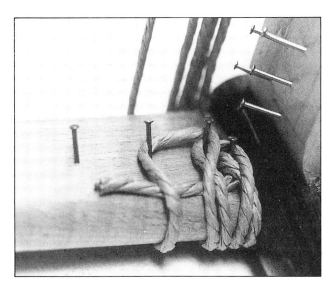

*The front loops are
a bit more
complicated.*

over the top of it, and back to the front rail to be looped round the first and second nails. Then down under and round the front rail, over the frame to the back to be looped round the second back nail, before being laid against itself on the underside of the rail and brought up on the outside to return to the front rail.

At the front rail it goes down the outside and under and up to loop over the second nail (not round it), next taken to the third nail where it is brought round towards the bottom of the rail, thus making a two-nail loop. It is then brought under and round the front rail and over the frame to the back.

Looping the cord over two nails at the front creates the space between the pairs of warp cords in which the wraps will be made. When laying the warp, allow a slight amount of slack in the cords before looping over the nails; it will be taken up in the weaving. Because of this slack the warp cords will wish to slide towards the middle of the front and back rails because of the saddle shape, but provided you initially lay them in their correct places on these two rails (i.e. directly over their respective nails) you will find that the wraps between each pair will bring them to their proper places.

Note that the first four warp cords have been laid side by side as two pairs; they will be woven as a single warp in the weaving.

At the back rail, the cord goes under and up the inside to loop round the next nail, then is brought down and over the back rail to the front rail. Here it is taken down round the rail, looped over the third nail on top of the previous coil, then brought sideways to go over the fourth nail before going once again under and round the front rail and to the back. Now the first pair of warp cords has been laid.

This sequence of looping over the nails at front and back in the two different ways is continued across the frame. Lay the last four cords side by side as you laid the first four. To finish the warp, take the final cord over the last nail in the right corner of the front rail and tack it to the front end of the right side rail, leaving about 2in (51mm) extending along the right side rail to be covered and held securely by the weft cords. Cut off the rest.

You will need about 12–13 yards (10.92–11.83m) of cord to form the wraps over the front rail, which are started from the middle of the frame. Loop the cord over the middle nail in the front rail so as to leave equal lengths of cord on each side. Take one end, loop it over itself below the nail and make the wraps between the pairs of warp cords towards the corner. The number of wraps between each pair will have been ascertained from the old seat before it was cut away from the frame. If the seat had already been removed, allow an average of four wraps between each pair of warp cords along the front rail, and three along the back. The aim is to keep each pair of warp cords centrally above their appropriate nails. This may call for sometimes five, sometimes three wraps between them; it does not really matter, so long as you copy the

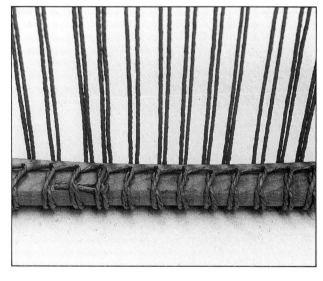

The inside of the front rail with the warp completed. Note the join left of centre in the illustraion. If a join has to be made, it is done as if you are beginning the warp. Lay the old end below the next few nails to be covered by the next few cords and lay the end of the new cord over the appropriate nail to be covered by the next loop.

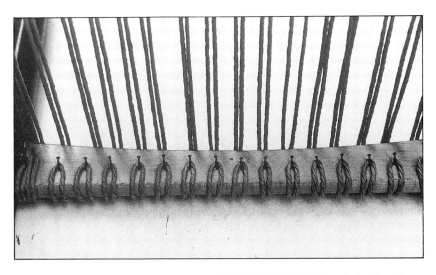

The inside of the back rail, warp completed.

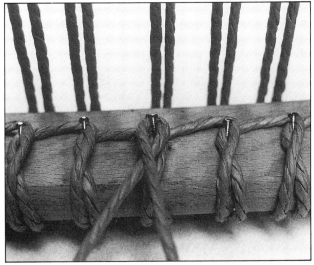

Starting the wraps from the centre of the inside of the front rail.

number of wraps between the same two pairs of warp cords on the other half of the front rail.

Having wrapped one half, proceed to wrap the next. Make sure that when the last cord of each set of wraps goes to start the next set between the next two pairs of warp cords, it crosses the warp cords on the inside of the rail and not underneath it. By the time you have finished wrapping, all cords should lie neatly and compactly against each other on the top, outside and underside of the

Starting the wraps on the back rail.

rail. Nail or tack the end of the wrap cord on the inside of the rail when wrapping has been completed, then loop it over the end nail to leave 2–3in (51–76mm) to be covered by the weft cords.

The back rail is wrapped in the same way as the front. For this, you will need only about 10–12 yards (9.1–10.92m) of cord for an average of three wraps between the pairs of warps. Secure the end as before.

When both front and back rails have been warped and wrapped, hammer home the nails in those two rails so that the loops are held fast. L-shaped nails should be hammered in straight; if you have used ordinary nails they must be bent over the cords so that their heads form hooks.

When weaving the seat you can start at the front or the back of the frame. I prefer to start at the back; the side rails slant towards the back, which encourages the weft cords to lie closer to each other; it is not quite so easy to keep them close up if you start at the front because they will want to slide towards the back. There is no need to cut a length of cord, as the weaving will be done with one continuous length without need to join. In fact it will be done with double cords, which means in theory that you should get it done in half the time!

In the same way that you started laying the warp, loop the end of the

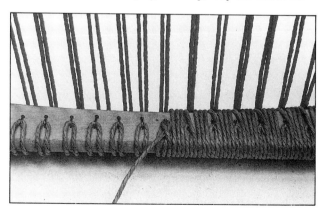

Half the back rail wraps are in place.

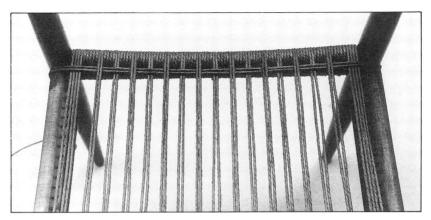

The first pair of weft cords is in place. As the work progresses, keep each weft as straight as possible. If this is not done, *there could be difficulty in getting them straight in the later stages of the weaving.*

cord over the first nail at the back of a side rail – it matters not which one – so that the weaving end goes over the short end and holds it firmly. Get used to weaving this seat with your fingers; there is enough space between the warp cord pairs to push through your finger and thumb to pick up the weaver, and this is quicker than having to thread the long needle each time. Only when you get close to the front rail with the weaving will you need some kind of help to pick up the cord; the long-nosed pliers are as good as anything.

Bring the cord out under the side rail and make a big loop about 3ft (91.4cm) long. Where the cord bends at the top of the loop is taken as the weaving end. Weave this double end of cord over the four warp cords at the side, then under and over alternate warp pairs to the other side,

finally going over the other four warp cords. The loop in the doubled cord is then taken over the rail and under it, to be looped in a clockwise direction over the first nail on the inside of that side rail at the back.

Before bedding the loop firmly on the nail, pull taut the cord which is nearest to the back; then loop it firmly over the nail, and pull the second cord of the pair taut towards the opposite frame. You will see that with one sequence of over and under movements you have automatically laid a double weft cord.

The cord is then pulled tightly round the rail close to the previous cords and looped over the first nail again, over the end of the previous cord. Make another big loop as before, but this time weave it under and over the warp cords – under the two pairs at the side, then over the next pair, under the next, contrarily to the first double weft cords. Cover the loose ends of cord lying along the inside of the rails as you work. Weave across the seat, round the rail, pull the first cord of this pair taut and loop it round the second nail on the other rail. Keep repeating this pattern of weaving – under and over, over and under alternately – until you reach the front of the seat. The last few rows of weaving will be rather tight, and it is necessary to pull the cords tight after every three or four weaves of the warp cords.

From time to time check that the pairs of weft cords are lying straight and parallel and next to each other; they should lie on the top of the rail, immediately above their respective nails. If they are not lying straight, compact them with the screwdriver and hammer; hold the screwdriver upright against the cords and tap them into their rightful position. Some bulging may occur in the weaving pattern, the centre of it advancing to the front faster than the two sides. Compact the cords by inserting the screwdriver between two pairs and tapping them back into place. Similarly, the warp cords may have been pulled out of alignment during the weaving, in which case tap them also back into line, but be careful not to let the blade of the screwdriver damage the cords as you do so.

Finish off by nailing a tack in a suitable position on the inside of the side rail so that the end of the cord can be looped round it from below and brought up to lie over two or three of the weft nails. Then, starting with the nails holding the end, hammer in all the nails in the side rails, and finally cut the cord close to the last anchoring nail.

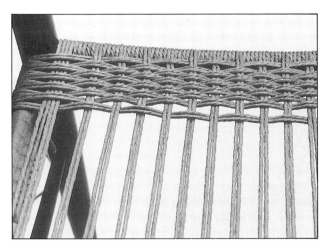

The top of the seat after 10 pairs of cords have been woven.

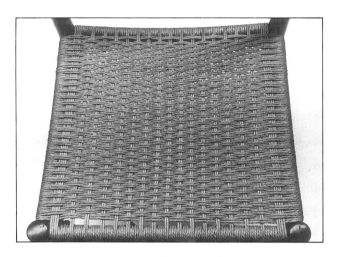

The finished seat.

There is another method of weaving with Danish cord on this particular design of chair – and also on stools – which does not entail the use of nails as hooks, though it does require a tension stick and shorter lengths of cord.

First mark on the top surface of the front rail where the warp cords are to lie – 4 at each end and 15 in between, equally spaced. Lay the tension stick across the middle of the side rails. Tie a knot about 2in (51mm) from the end of the cord and nail through it into the inside of the front rail against the left corner. Take the cord under the rail and round it, then over it and across over the tension stick to the back rail; take it up on the inside between the cord and the corner, loop it over itself and then back down the inside of the rail to go under and up on the outside. Thread it through the loop made over the cord and bring it back to the front rail, the two cords lying side by side. Lay it round over the front rail and then up inside the frame between the first cord and the corner, and loop it over both cords. This has made a pair of warp cords with a loop at each end.

Take the cord down under and over the front rail and across to the back; up on the inside of the rail between the second and third cords, then loop it over itself and back down under the rail to come up the outside and be threaded through the loop over the third cord. Bring it back to the front rail, down the outside, up on the inside between the second and third cords, and loop it over the second pair of cords. Your side warp of four cords has now been formed.

Now make a suitable number of short wraps round the front rail before bringing the cord up the outside of the rail where you have

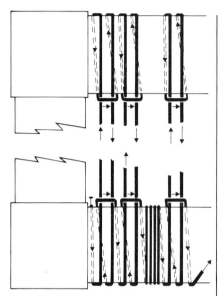

Warping with cord using the looped cord method.

marked the position of the first of the pairs of warp cords. As before, take the cord to the back rail, round it, and loop it over itself on the mark for the first pair of warp cords on the back rail. Then take it back down and under and over the top to thread through that loop, and bring it forward to the front. Take it down under the front rail and up between the first cord of this pair and the four cords at the side, and loop it over both cords of this latest pair. The first pair of warp cords has now been laid.

Wrap a few times round the front rail again, and make the next warp pair of cords over the next mark on the top of front and back rails.

Loops and wraps on a rail. Make sure that each cord lies snugly against its neighbours. If it over-rides (as in the centre of this illustration) it will create an unsightly bump and will be difficult to tease into its correct position when the work is finished. Moreover, the work will be fractionally loose at this point as the cord will have had to be stretched to get the recalcitrant wrap into place.

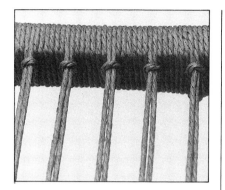

What the warp should look like from above.

Continue in this way to the right side rail, wrapping round the front rail only. Make the loops at front and back rails in the same way each time – by bringing the cord up between the last pair of cords and the pair being laid, and looping over towards the right side rail. Press all loops against the rail so that they are uniform. Nail the end of the last wrap to the inside of the front rail close to the corner, and let 2–3in (51–76mm) lie loosely to be covered by the weft cords.

To wrap the back rail, make a knot some 2in (51mm) from the end of a new cord and nail through it into the back rail on the right, adjacent to the inner cord of the four-cord warp, leaving the end to be covered by the short wraps. Bring the cord under the back rail and up the outside to wrap as many times as necessary between each pair of warp cords without shifting them from their positions

over their marks. When crossing the warp loops from one set of wraps to the next, make sure that the cross is on the inside of the rail and not underneath, so that all cords lie smoothly against each other. When the wraps reach the other end of the back rail, knock a short nail into the inside of the rail against the four-cord wrap, loop the wrap cord round it and hammer it home to grip the cord firmly. Then bring the cord under the side rail at the back, ready to begin weaving.

The weft is made in the same way as the warp – by taking the cord across to the opposite rail and round it to come up on the inside between the cord and the corner, where it is looped over itself and brought down and under the rail, over the top and through the loop, and woven across to the other rail. The weaving sequence is the same: over the first four cords, under and over alternate pairs, and over the last four; round the rail and up on the inside between the cord and the corner, looped over itself and brought down and round the outside of the rail, then threaded through the loop and back in the same over and under sequence to the opposite rail where it comes up between the previous cord and the corner, to be looped over both before coming up on the outside for the reverse weave (under and over, where before it was over and under).

The joining of old with new cords in this method is done by making a knot at the end of each. Ease the loops of two or three pairs of cords away from the rail, so that the new end can be passed through between the cords and the rail. Tie a knot in the end of the cord to prevent it from slipping out, and pull the cord so that the knot is resting against a warp cord. Twist the new cord a couple of times with the old and lay about 3in (76mm) of the old cord along the inside of the rail with a knot at the end, to be covered by the weft cords still to be looped round the rail. Joins may need to be made on the side rails, but there should be no necessity for them on the front and back if you work with long continuous warp and wrap cords; if they should be required, they are made in the same way.

To finish, hammer a short nail into the inside of the rail at which the final cord ends, so that the cord can be looped round it and the nail hammered over it to hold it in place. For added security, another nail may be placed 1–2in (25–51mm) further along the rail, to be hammered over the cord a second time.

With this method the weaving pattern will not be as close as in the previous one, as the side rail loops will prevent the weft cords from lying close against each other. It will make a more open weave.

With a little integrity more elaborate patterns can be worked with Danish cord on rectangular and square stools too. If you wish to try another ready-made pattern, that described for the second method in the section on Binder Cane looks very attractive (*see* page 135).

A combination of the two methods is obtained by looping the warp ends over themselves as in the second method, but using the first method of looping over nails in the side rails for the weft. This also gives a stronger seat than if both warp and weft cords were looped over themselves without using the nails.

3
CANING TECHNIQUES

WHAT IS CHAIR SEATING CANE?

Cane chair seating originated in the Far East – some authorities say in China, some say India. Be that as it may, such chairs were being made and seats woven many centuries before trade brought them to Europe. It is thought that Catherine of Braganza, who became Charles II's Queen Consort, introduced the first caned chairs into England from Portugal's eastern trading areas, or from Portugal itself; Portuguese furniture makers were at the height of their skills in the latter half of the seventeenth century. It was during the early years of Charles II's reign that the early, very coarse cane work gave way to more delicate weaving techniques. This became the new fashion in furniture for England and her colonies – including America, which imported quantities of caned chairs from England.

More skilful techniques in the making of furniture meant that more craftsmen were needed, especially those with greater abilities, and London quickly became the Mecca for Dutch and French craftsmen whose skills were at that time greater than those available in England. But London furniture makers and weavers of cane seats learned quickly; and not only in London – apparently chair makers in the rural districts around the capital also saw their opportunities and helped to satisfy the demand.

It was the Great Fire of London in 1666 which hastened the improvement in the appearance and comfort of English furniture. So many of the capital's old timber houses having been destroyed, there was a demand for more substantial buildings of stone and brick designed also to give more interior space. To furnish these more spacious rooms, whose decoration was far more ornate than English families had been accustomed to, the bulkier solid furniture which had been obligatory for so long gave way to pieces which were more in keeping. There followed very closely, almost hand in hand, a distinction being made between those rooms set aside for entertaining and others constituting domestic quarters for private daily use.

Strange as it may seem, the cane chairs which became so fashionable during the period after the Great Fire were imported from France and

Holland into London's less ostentatious homes – those whose families had hitherto been accustomed only to uncomfortable stools and benches – and often consisted of sets of six or eight single chairs and two armchairs. Unfortunately, according to the aesthetic standards of our own century, the basic simplicity of the design of these chairs was lost when the fashionable furniture makers of the day took an interest and persuaded the occupants of the larger houses that cane work, particularly cane chairs, was the latest thing. This was unfortunate because the comparative simplicity of design and comfort of the imported chairs was lost in increasingly elaborate decoration. Higher backs, spiral turning and flamboyant carving were features much in keeping with Charles II's reign.

Quantities of cane-seated chairs were ordered for the official residences of Charles II and James II, but although popular from the start with their lowlier subjects these were not accepted into the private apartments of the royal households until the time of William and Mary.

It is hardly surprising that the popularity of cane chairs gave upholsterers and the manufacturers of the more traditional chairs cause for alarm. Towards the end of the century they petitioned Parliament (unsuccessfully) to ban the import and manufacture of chairs with cane seats and backs.

Nevertheless, despite the failure of the petition, by the turn of the century the popularity of cane furniture was on the wane, although it was still being made well into the next century. Indeed, some of the tallest chairs ever seen in England were made in the closing years of the seventeenth century, with cane-panelled backs nearly 4ft (1.21m) higher than the cane seats.

Some of the greatest furniture designers advocated the use of cane work. Thus Chippendale, in his *Gentleman and Cabinet-Maker's Directory* of 1754, affirmed that 'such chairs are very proper for a Lady's Dressing Room, They have commonly Cane-Bottoms with loose Cushions but if required may have stuffed Seats and Brass Nails.' Similarly, Sheraton (1751–1806), whose *The Cabinet Maker and Upholsterer's Drawing-Book* had a marked influence on the trade, urged the revival of cane-work seats for parlour and drawing room chairs.

Though it was another 200 years before cane work regained the popularity it had enjoyed in the latter part of the seventeenth century, it has always had its place in the designers' portfolios. After Nelson's victory at the Battle of Trafalgar in 1805, a particularly graceful chair was designed and known as the 'Trafalgar' type, so called – it has been suggested – because of its sabre front legs and the rope mouldings on its back uprights and top rail. The cane seat and small rectangular cane panel in the back typify this style, which has many variations including the bergère with caned seat, sides and back. Even so, upholsterers still kept their feet in the door: these 'Trafalgars' and bergères frequently had squab cushions on the seats.

The appeal of lightweight domestic furniture was considerable: chairs that could be carried from one end to another of a library or smoking room, parlour, withdrawing room – any room where conversation was to be a part of the social scene – were greatly in demand. This kind of 'aid to mobility' in the home was given even greater impetus by the import and manufacture in England of papier-mâché furniture, lightweight in construction and made even lighter by the frequent use of cane seating.

In the middle of the last century cane-seated lightweight furniture really took off, thanks to the genius of Michael Thonet, the inventor of mass-produced bentwood chairs. Thonet, the most innovative designer and maker of furniture in the nineteenth century, was born at Boppard-am-Rhein in 1796 and began his experiments in 1830, first with veneers and laminations bent in moulds, but these were not too successful. His primary objective was to find a means of economizing on materials and labour. He interested Prince Metternich (Austria's foreign minister) in his ideas, and moved to Vienna in 1842 under the Prince's patronage, setting up a factory there seven years later where he concentrated on bending wood (usually beech) by steam or boiling water in wooden moulds. He also developed a process whereby chairs could be made in marked parts and assembled on arrival at their destination. Thonet exhibited at the Great Exhibition in London in 1851, and within 10 years his cheap, simply designed cane-seated chairs were being sent all over the world. Many Victorian homes, shops and hotels had them, as did Viennese restaurants, Australian cafés and American hotels. In the 20 years until his death in 1871, his factory was producing up to 400,000 such pieces of furniture annually.

One still comes across bentwood chairs from the Victorian era, more often than not without their caned seats. Victorian mamas decided that slouching in a chair was unhygienic for their offspring, bad for deportment and not socially acceptable. Comfortable though such chairs are, they were thought to produce round shoulders and curvature of the spine. Parents wanted to put the clock back and reintroduce hard, solid, uncomfortable seats for their children at table and in the nursery, hence the large number of parlour chairs still around with varnished plywood seats patterned with ventilating holes, nailed on to the seat frame although the cane seat beneath was still in good condition.

During the period between the two World Wars, craftsmen who could re-weave a cane seat became fewer. Apart from their seats, the chairs made by Thonet were in good condition, but with no one around to carry out repairs plywood seats were affixed to the seat-frame instead. Furthermore, the fashion for cane-work chairs once again faded towards the end of the nineteenth century and they remained relatively unwanted for the best part of 60 years, despite the attempts at the manufacture of graceful cane furniture by Dryad Works, founded in 1907 following experiments by B. J. Fletch and Charles Crampton at the Leicester Art School.

The making of rattan furniture from the pulp (better known in Britain as centre cane) of the rattan palm had been made a commercial possibility by the experiments of an American, Cyrus Wakefield, in the 1850s. Until then this inner pulp had usually been thrown away as having no worthwhile use, but Wakefield set up a factory in Massachusetts specifically to make rattan furniture and invented the method of cutting cane by machine. At about the same time, also in America, Gardiner A. Watkins is believed to have invented the machinery to weave cane mechanically into panels.

One of the more esoteric uses to which this machine-woven cane was put was as decorative panels on the sides of the bodywork of some sporty-looking motor cars. Of greater importance was the utilization of pre-woven panels in the design of chromium-plated tubular steel chairs, with seat frames and back panels of wood into which these panels are impressed. This type of chair was originally designed about 1925 by Mies van der Rohe and Marcel Breuer, working in Germany, and remains extremely popular today. Their experimental prototypes of furniture made of tubular steel owed much to Thonet, who had pioneered the mass production of elegant and cheap machine-made furniture for a wide market.

There was a danger of the craft of chair-seat weaving with rattan cane dying out completely in Europe from the outbreak of the Second World War. Imports of cane from the Far East had naturally ceased in 1939, and it was well into the 1950s before the demand re-established itself and British craftspeople mastered the skills and techniques to get it going again. Since then, fashion has decreed that once again the cane chair seat should be included in every discerning home.

The uses of the plant from which we get our cane for chair seating are extraordinarily varied. In the Far East, it has been used for centuries for making rough baskets, huts, furniture, suspension bridges, traps for fish, traps for elephants, sleeping mats – in addition to its more recent uses in the manufacture of whips, hampers, bat and tennis racket handles, stiffening in the peaks of military hats. In fact, we chair seaters use only a very small proportion of the plant.

Rattans are jungle creepers reaching a length of up to 500ft (152m) in the steamy forests of the Far East, varying in thickness from a few millimetres to the size of a human arm (though the thickness of each plant is constant throughout its length). Some canes can be found in other tropical countries, such as West Africa, but these varieties are not a patch on those to be found in the forests of South-East Asia, specifically in the Malay Peninsula, Indonesia and the Philippines, where they are generally considered to be a secondary product. Though there is a limited amount of commercial cultivation, in the main the plant grows naturally.

Trade in rattan has become a multi-billion-dollar business. However, extremely worried by the increasing commercial exploitation of cane in recent years – resulting in forest supplies being in grave danger of exhaustion in the foreseeable future – South-East Asian governments and individuals have been desperately seeking ways of conserving and propagating the endangered species. Diminishing forest cover and uncontrolled exploitation have depleted rattans throughout the area to the point where the trades connected with it are on the verge of collapse. Rattan plantations are not yet able to satisfy the demand for cane.

Much of the split cane that we use for chair seating is exported from Malaysia to Germany, where it is prepared before being imported into the UK in the form we know it. The rest of our needs comes mainly through Singapore.

There are approximately 600 species in 14 genera, most of which are suitable for cane products of some kind or other, but the two with which we are concerned belong to the genera *Calamus* and *Daemonoropos*. (Bamboo is not a member of the family; bamboo has a distinctive node at the point from where the leaf grew, while rattan has a rough edge there.)

The rattan palm grows vertically until it reaches a height of 2–3ft

(61–91.4cm), after which it is supported by long tendrils which attach themselves to other vegetation. In fact, the word 'tendril' is likely to give the wrong impression, for these feelers are nothing like those which are put out by the convolvulus or ivy, though they serve the same purpose. The rattan's tendril's are vicious: like the plant's outer bark they are covered with strong, sharp thorns, far worse than any bramble we encounter in our hedgerows. These cruelly barbed tendrils grow for up to 18in (45.7cm) from the tip of the leaves, which themselves have little sharp spikes along the underside of the main vein. Altogether an unpleasant plant to encounter in its natural state!

Nevertheless, that is where our seating cane comes from; and just like any other crop of use to man, it has to be harvested. It is hardly surprising that the local workers prefer to harvest the crop only when no less hazardous employment is available. Wearing thick hide gloves to protect their hands from the thorns, they begin by cutting the rattan vines with axes to about 3ft (91.4cm) from the ground; this allows new growth to get established, which will be ready for harvesting six or seven years later. The creepers are then left to hang in order that the sun can shrivel and loosen the outer bark. After some days the workers return to strip the outer bark from the stem; this is traditionally done by pulling the creeper through a notch they have cut into the trunk of a convenient nearby tree, or twisting it round a tree trunk to remove the leaves and outer bark (with its thorns) by friction. Occasionally, if the plant has hooked itself by its thorns particularly firmly into other vegetation, a worker has to climb up to cut it loose.

Once the outer bark, leaves and thorns have been removed, the inner bark is revealed – a hard, glossy silicious surface covering the central pith. The cane is cut into lengths of between 12ft (3.64m) and 30ft (9.12m), tied in bundles and taken immediately – before the stems begin to deteriorate – to the nearest processing yard for curing. There it is subjected to sulphuration in order to destroy any fungi and insects.

The next stage in the preparation of the cane is its grading by quality and diameter. As both these vary considerably, the individual lengths are further scrutinized – for smoothness, colour, length of joints between leaf nodes, etc. – before being passed mechanically through a machine which separates the central core, or pith, from the glossy inner bark. The central core is further processed to become the centre cane used for so much of our cane basketwork craft activities in Britain and America.

The inner bark is next split and trimmed by razor-sharp knives, either by hand or mechanically, into flat strips of about $\frac{1}{16}$in (1.5mm) thickness, now recognizable as the basic material for our chair seating and wrapping. Before being sold direct to manufacturers or to dealers in Singapore and Hong Kong for despatch to Europe and America, the final step in the processing is a further trimming of each strand to ensure uniform thickness and width.

The predominant use of cane in the factories is for weaving by special looms into cane webbing, also referred to as pre-woven or machine-woven cane or manufactured cane chair seating. Strictly speaking, this webbing is not completely machine-woven for the open-weave (chair seating) panels: the diagonals are woven-in by hand, the loom attendant using a specially made spiral tool of metal, something like an elongated corkscrew. Cane webbing made in this way is up to 36in (91.4cm) in width, in rolls of 50ft (15.2m). The looms also weave close canework. Because of the labour-intensive nature of traditional hand-woven cane seats and panels, virtually all contemporary furniture manufacturers incorporating such seats and panels now utilize cane webbing.

PREPARATION FOR WORK

Before taking up the first strand of cane to begin weaving, there is work to be done. The old seat or panel must be removed and the frame cleaned completely.

You may find it useful to make a rough sketch of the old pattern, particularly if the canework looks complicated round the edges. On your sketch, give every hole in each rail a consecutive number, so that you can refer to it in order to get the strands in the right holes. Once you have removed the old caning it is difficult to copy direct from it because where the pattern matters – along the rails – will have been cut off. However, the old work may have been badly caned in the first place, in which case it will be a waste of time to try to copy it. The criterion by which to judge whether or not the old frame was properly woven is primarily an aesthetic one at this stage. If the pattern itself is consistent all over the frame – if the diagonals, horizontals and vertical strands are all in straight lines over the main body of the work, if the work looks pleasing in its symmetry – then it is fairly safe to say that the weaving was well done.

The tools and equipment you will require are few and simple. Most of them can be found in the kitchen and in the toolbox, but should you have any difficulty they are available from most handicraft shops. Alternatively, you can easily improvise with some of them.

It may seem trite to state that the most important tools are your fingers; nevertheless that is perfectly true. They do most of the work, but they have to be supplemented by:

▌Small hammer
▌Sharp knife, e.g. penknife blade
▌Pair of side cutters or small but strong scissors (toenail scissors are ideal)
▌Hand drill
▌Small stiletto, bodkin, or awl with a sharp point
▌Pair of long-nosed pliers to assist in removing pieces of old cane
▌Clearer, to punch the old pegs from their holes (a nail of diameter slightly less than the frame holes, with the point blunted, makes an excellent substitute)
▌Pegs about 2in (51mm) in length, cut from round centre cane of suitable diameter; golf tees are often used as temporary pegs
▌Container for water
▌Old towel, some rag and a sponge
▌Supplies of chair seating cane
▌Some small elastic bands

Seating cane is generally available in 250g hanks. This is the most economical way of buying it if you are planning to weave a number of seats or panels, but small packets containing sufficient for a single seat are sold by handicraft shops or by mail order.

The sizes of seating cane range from the finest (No. 0) which is used only in the most delicate work and measures a mere $1/16$in (1.3mm) in width, up to No. 6 size ($3/16$in or 3.7mm wide), each intermediate size increasing by about 0.4mm. No. 6 cane is the most common size for the beading, while Nos. 2 and 3 (approximately $3/32$in or 2.1mm and $7/64$in or 2.5mm) are usual for an ordinary cane seat. If you are satisfied that the seat you have cut away was made of the right sizes of cane by someone who knew their craft, you can take it to a handicraft shop where they will be able to match and supply the correct sizes.

The relationship between the diameter of the frame holes and the distance between them determines the size or sizes of cane to be used in the six-way standard method of cane weaving. This is by far the most common pattern, and also the strongest. Though this relationship between diameter and distance of frame holes is of importance to chair makers constructing a frame for caning, for all practical purposes it is sufficient to be guided by the chart below. First, measure a distance of 6in (15.2cm) from the centre of any hole in either of the side rails, and count the number of holes in that 6in (15.2cm) stretch (side rail holes are more likely to be evenly spaced than those in the back and front rails).

No. of holes	10	11	12	13
Cane size	4	3 & 4	3	2 & 3

No. of holes	14	15	16
Cane size	2	1 & 2	1

In any pair of sizes in the chart, the larger size of cane is invariably used for the diagonal weaving strands in the six-way standard pattern.

Using a pair of sturdy scissors or a sharp knife, cut away the old cane close to the inside of the rails without damaging the woodwork. Turn the chair so that you can get to the reverse of the seat or panel, and sever the loops between the holes on the other side. Take care not to nick the wood: a hallmark of a good cane weaver is as much the neatness of the unseen part of his work as the elegance of the visible pattern.

Any beading covering the holes round the frame must be removed by cutting through the finer cane which sews the beading through the holes (called the couching cane) and pulling the beading away. The holes which have been pegged will be revealed.

Most, if not all, of the holes in the rails will have been pegged, and these pegs have to be removed by gentle tapping with the hammer on the clearer, preferably from beneath: the pegs were originally inserted from above, and their easiest way out is upwards. Sometimes the dust and dirt of ages has effectively stuck them to the holes and the only way to remove such pegs is by drilling them out with a hand drill. Drill from the top downwards, just in case you should drill out of true and the hole becomes enlarged at the other end. You will need to take particular care with some antique chairs, in which the frame holes were drilled at alternate angles. In a well-made frame for caning, there is a definite relationship between the distance between the holes and their diameter.

Once the last vestige of old cane has been removed from all the holes, pegged and unpegged, there will doubtless be bits of fluff and dirt adhering to the inside of the rails. The wood of the frame where the canework has covered it will have become discoloured. All this has to be cleaned up. In fact, any treatment and repairs to the chair itself – and not only to the rails – should be carried out before the weaving begins.

A not uncommon problem arises where the frame holes have been split along part of the rail. This may have been caused by too-large pegs having been driven into the holes, or because with age the wood has become weaker than the cane of the weaving. I have not come across any reference to tests on the breaking strain of a strand of cane, but this must be quite considerable. At least four strands go into each hole, so it is understandable that the canework – particularly if the seat has been re-woven since the chair was made – can be stronger than the wood supporting it. Whatever the reason, consider carefully if the split can be repaired. If the split is not too bad, the edges can be brought together by screwing laterally from the inside of the frame at intervals between holes. In this way the split can be reduced to such an extent that the diameter of the holes is virtually unimpaired. If this does not prove effective, you will have to decide whether it is worth the time and trouble to undertake the major job of replacing the entire rail.

Another minor repair job has to be done where a hitherto caned seat has at some time had a shaped piece of perforated plywood tacked on to the frame. Bentwood dining chairs have been particularly susceptible to this treatment in the past, and frequently it is found that the tacks have penetrated the wood of the frame on the outside of the holes. Having removed the plywood, the tack holes must be filled in and the frame renovated before the canework is begun.

Before use, the cane has to be made pliable. It is best to store it when not being used in a dark, cool place, where it should not be allowed to dry out. Dry cane is likely to become brittle, resulting in splits and breaks and lack of elasticity, so it must be dampened immediately before use and kept damp while you are

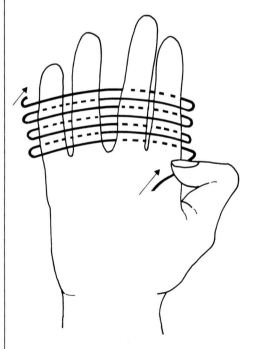

Making a skein of cane; the starting end is held by the thumb against the base of the first finger.

working with it. Prepare a few long strands by coiling each separately and holding them in place with an elastic band. Or make skeins of them: hold the end of a strand between your thumb joint and base of your forefinger, wrap the strand over the first two fingers, bring it towards the palm of your hand between your second and third fingers, wrap round your third and fourth fingers, up and through towards your palm between your second and third fingers, and carry on.

A lot of seemingly contradictory advice is given about how long the cane should be soaked and what temperature the water should be. One expert may recommend leaving it for 15 minutes in a bowl of water which is at a temperature of around 120°F (50°C) and using it straight away. Another may advocate placing it in cold water for two minutes and wrapping it in a wet towel for a further 15 minutes before use. A third states that soaking in tepid water for half an hour is the best way. Each may be right, according to the quality and size of the cane and the temperature and humidity in which they are working. All I can say, from my own experience over many years, is that on a hot summer day I need only dip the coil of No. 2 cane into a bowl of cold water for a few seconds; about a minute for No. 6 cane. I then place it in a small transparent plastic bag, which I seal so that the moisture cannot escape, until I am ready to use it (usually within half an hour). But on a warm autumn morning after a humid night during which the cane has absorbed moisture from the atmosphere, I can use it without any preparation apart from keeping it wrapped in a moist towel until I am ready to handle it. On a cold day in midwinter with my workshop temperature around 60°F, I let No. 2 cane lie in warm water (mainly to prevent my hands from being too cold) for half a minute and use it at once. Larger sizes I leave in the water a little longer.

On balance, it is better for the cane to be just damp rather than soaking wet. Cane which is left in water for any length of time goes blackish, loses its gloss and develops splits along its length.

If you are working in a warm room the cane will dry out sooner rather than later, so always have a damp sponge handy to keep moist not only the strand you are weaving with but also that part of the work which you have already woven. To weave a damp strand over work which is dry causes the weaving strand to undulate unnecessarily; damp strands yield to each other.

One last point before you begin weaving – get into the habit of drawing each strand between your forefinger and thumb immediately before you start to weave it. Every 18in (45.7cm) or so along there is a node (where the base of the leaf grew in its natural forest state). With your thumbnail, feel for these nodes; if it catches against the nodes as you are pulling the strand through, you will know that will be the wrong direction in which to pull it as you weave, for if it catches against your nail it will just as surely catch against the other strands and encourage them to break.

SIX-WAY STANDARD PATTERN

The most common pattern in cane seating is known generally as the six-way standard. This gives the strongest seat, each strand locking into position those which have already been laid. Other patterns can be just as decorative, but are more often used for side and back panels which do not have so much weight put upon them.

Having decided on the correct sizes of cane to be used and with the cane suitably prepared by dampening, examine the seat itself. There is invariably the same number of holes in each of the two side rails; whether it is an odd or even number of holes is not important. Not so with the back and front rails, however, unless the seat is square or rectangular. The front rail being longer than the back, there will usually be more holes in it, and ideally there should be an odd or an even number in each of these two rails. If there is an odd number in one and an even number in the other, there is a minor difficulty but nothing to worry about.

Each step of the work is known by a name; *Step 1* (sometimes called the *First Setting* or *First Vertical*) consists of laying the first strands of what is in effect the warp, the seat being regarded as the loom in this weaving process.

Place a peg in the hole in the middle of the back rail, and another in the middle hole at the front. Should there be an even number of holes, place a peg in the hole to the left of where the central hole would have been had there been an odd number of holes. If there is an odd number of holes in one rail and an even number in the other, peg the middle hole of the rail in which there is an odd number. In the opposite rail, carefully measure with a rule to find the middle, and then place a peg in the hole nearest to it. These two pegs are for reference when you start caning.

After removing the peg in the back rail, feed a strand through that hole until about half its length is above and half below the hole. Insert a peg to hold it in position firmly, but not so firmly that you will have difficulty in getting it out. This is temporary pegging and will occur throughout the weaving process, the pegs being removed whenever another strand has to be fed through the holes. The glossy side of the cane is upper-most – ánd must always be, whether it is above or on the underside of the frame. Always let the weaving strand run through your fingers to ensure that the glossy side is uppermost and to avoid twisting the strand.

The end coming up out of the hole is then threaded down through the corresponding pegged hole in the front rail (i.e. the middle one, or the left one of the middle two), and pegged. Do not pull the strand too tight, but allow a little slack. But how slack is slack? This is a matter of preference, and while some weavers place a stick across the two side rails and weave over it, others – like

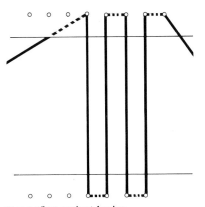

Step 1 (first setting) begins.

myself – rely on the 'feel' of the tension by placing the palm of the hand on the weaving as it progresses.

Now feed the strand under the rail to right or left (it matters not) and up through the next hole. Hold the strand tightly against the underside of the rail with your finger or thumb, and secure it with the peg before taking the cane across to the corresponding hole in the back rail – again letting it run through your fingers to make sure it is still glossy side up and not twisted. Get into the habit of doing this with every movement until it becomes second nature to you.

Put the strand through the next hole in the back rail and insert a new peg – not the one you first put in: the removal of that would make the first vertical strand go slack. Place the flat of your hand on both these strands to test that they have the same amount of tension; keep doing this throughout this step of the weaving, because too much tension will make the final weaving steps extremely difficult. Now bring the strand up through the next hole.

Continue until every back rail hole in this half of the frame has a strand in it, with the exception of the corner hole. The strand is threaded down through the last hole in the back rail, pegged, and cut off beneath the frame so as to leave 3in or 4in (76mm– 102mm) hanging.

Then take the other end of the strand, which is hanging through the hole in the middle of the rail, and proceed in precisely the same manner in the opposite direction, towards the other back corner.

Before every hole in the back rail has a strand in it, it is likely that another length of cane will have to be added. To join a new strand, bring the last few inches of the previous strand up through the next hole, and insert the new end down it. The end of the new strand is threaded under the loop made beneath the rail, then back and under itself to make a single knot. The ends of every knot should point towards the inside of the seat. Knots are centred between two holes on the underside, pulled tight, and then tapped flat to make a neat join. Take good care to see that the new

strand is sufficiently damp, otherwise it is likely to be split or break. Some caners prefer to leave the ends of both old and new strands pegged firmly in the same hole, postponing the tying of the two ends until the whole of the seat has been woven. It is a matter of personal preference.

When removing an old caned panel from the back of a large piece of furniture, such as a settee, you may find that two strands have been knotted together during the actual weaving. Such a knot is not recommended. It is a special weaving knot, and it is better to use a new length of cane joined at the frame by knotting in the customary way, even if it means a few feet of cane have to be cut off. Those short lengths can often be utilized in the weaving of a smaller area.

Step 1 completed. Note the shorter strands from the front rail into side rail holes, maintaining the equidistance and parallel of the rest of the strands.

As it is usual for chair seats to have the front rail longer than the back, once the holes in the back rail have been completed with strands there will be some unfilled holes in the front. The method therefore is to continue threading the cane through the holes in the front rail, but to use some of the holes in the side rails. Shorter strands are woven from the spare front rail holes into suitable holes in the side rails, parallel to and equidistant from the strands already in position. Do not try to take the cane underneath the frame beyond the next adjacent hole to come to the surface, but cut it off underneath leaving 3in or 4in (76mm–102mm) hanging; then peg both ends firmly. Try not to let the strands on top cover other side holes, or you may have difficulty in threading through later strands. Also, the four corner holes should be left empty for the time being: they will be used in Steps 5 and 6.

For *Step 2* (or the *First Weaving* or *First Horizontal*), start by pegging a new strand of cane in the hole in the right side rail which is next to the back corner hole. This step is carried out in precisely the same way as *Step 1,* except that the strand is taken horizontally instead of vertically, the cane being laid over the vertical strands. Continue testing for tension with the palm of your hand; strands should not be slacker or tighter than

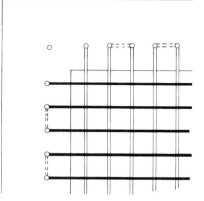

Step 2 (first weaving), laid over first setting at back left corner of seat.

the strands of *Step 1.* If some of the side rail holes have been pegged, remove each peg before threading the new strand through the hole, then replace it. There being an equal number of holes in each of the side rails, there will be no spare holes to weave into. The four corner holes are still not used.

If you are working on a bow-fronted seat, you may need to miss one or two holes between the last one or two weavings at the front of the seat, in order to keep the horizontal strands equidistant. Of course, if the seat is curved or bowed at the front corner there are often no obvious corner holes. (*See* Bow-fronted Frames, page 93.)

With a curved front rail, if the space between the last horizontal strand at the front and the middle holes in the rail is greater than the distance between the rest of the horizontal

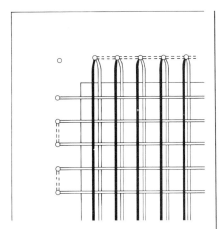

Step 3 (second setting), laid to left of first setting and over first weaving.

strands, then an additional strand or two has to be added, parallel to and as far as possible equidistant from the last horizontal strand between the two side rails. Use shorter strands for these, and peg each end.

Step 3 (*Second Setting* or *Second Vertical*) repeats *Step 1* (vertical) and is laid over the first two steps. It is necessary to ensure that the strands in this step lie to the left of those already in each hole, to facilitate later stages of the work. Start by inserting a new strand down through a front rail hole through which the strand in *Step 1* came up, and peg it. Take it back to the corresponding hole in the back rail, down through it, peg, and up through the next hole to the right. Continue as for *Step 1.* You will be reversing the direction of the threading, so new loops will be formed on the underside of the frame which will make later weaving easier and give a more professional look to the finished work. Short strands are laid at the sides. Make sure that the strands of *Step 3* lie to the left of those of *Step 1* on the top of the front and back rails. Keep testing for tension with the palm of your hand.

Now the work begins to get really interesting with Step 4 (*Second Weaving*

Step 2 completed. Note the extra short strand at the back of the frame and the two short ones at the front.

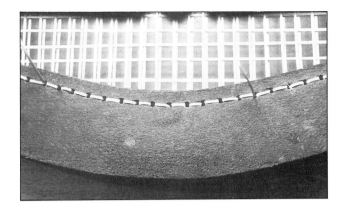

When Step 3 is completed, the underside of the frame should have looped strands between every hole. This neatness is a sign of good weaving.

Start Step 4 from the back of the frame, though for ease of weaving in the final stages of this step, shorter strands at the front can be woven first if the front rail is curved.

or *Second Horizontal*). This repeats *Step 2* (but in reverse, as *Step 3* was to *Step 1*), and is the first actual weaving you will do. It is imperative to get this step right, otherwise the rest of the weaving may not work properly. It is vital that all strands (not just the one being woven) are kept damp throughout this step, to avoid a wavy effect being caused by the supple new strand as it is woven through the stiff

dry strands of *Steps 1* and *3*. Start at the back of the seat, but if there is a short strand or strands at the front, weave these first; it is much easier to do this now than if you work them when you reach the back of the seat, because of the increasing tension of the work.

Peg a short strand into the same hole as the left end of the shortest horizontal strand at the front. Weave over the vertical of *Step 3* and under the vertical of *Step 1*, and above, i.e. further from the front rail than the existing short horizontal strand of *Step 2*. The recommended way of weaving is to have one hand below the weaving and the other above it, so as to feed the end of the cane over and under from one hand to the other.

When all the short strands at the front have been woven, peg a long strand into the hole on the left side rail at the back, opposite where the first long strand of *Step 2* went in – the direction of this horizontal weave is reversed, as in *Step 3*, to create matching loops on the underside. The new strand weaves over the vertical of *Step 1* and under the vertical of *Step 3*, and always above (nearer the back than the horizontal strands of

Step 2) across to the opposite rail, through that hole and up the next. Continue from front to back, pegging and joining as necessary, and ensuring that the new strand being woven does not lie on top of the existing strand, but as far as possible next to it as it enters or leaves the side holes. Do not weave more than six of the vertical pairs at once, and pull each strand as you weave until it is reasonably taut (but obviously not to breaking point!).

Before starting the next step, carefully straighten all the horizontal and vertical rows of caning so that they are parallel, each pair is as close together as possible, and the squares formed by the weaving so far are clearly defined. You can do this by using two pegs and pressing the strands together, or preferably with

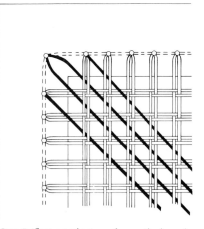

Step 4 (second weaving), laid over second setting and under first setting, and above first weaving.

Step 5 (first crossing), under verticals and over horizontals.

your thumb and forefinger, although if you are not used to it this could make them sore.

Step 5 (*First Crossing* or *First Diagonal*) needs particular care. Start by inserting and pegging a new strand into the back left corner hole. Weave over the horizontals and under the verticals. Do not try to weave the complete diagonal at one go; try weaving through four or five squares and pulling the whole length through. Remember to keep the whole of the weaving damp, not only the strand you are weaving with.

Continue down to the bottom right corner. Unless it is a square seat frame you are working on, it is most unlikely that it will go into the bottom right corner hole. Instead, it should be threaded through whichever hole is nearest to form a straight diagonal, whether this hole happens to be in the front or the side rail. Take the strand down that hole, and up the next to the left (if on the front rail) or below it (if on the side rail). At this stage you may begin to experience difficulty in getting the new strand through the holes, which

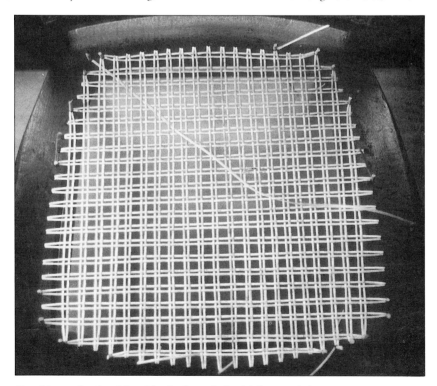

Step 4 is completed and Step 5 begins from the back left corner holes.

The correct way of interweaving the diagonals.

The wrong way to weave the diagonals. Note how the strand snags against the verticals and horizontals: it will never lie straight and will eventually wear at these points.

by now already have two strands in each. Simply ease a path through for it with a bodkin or fine awl.

Continue by weaving back the way you have come, to the back left corner, still going over the horizontals and under the verticals, until you reach the hole in the left side rail below the corner hole. Ease the strand through this, and up through the next hole along. Carry on weaving diagonally in this way until all the left triangle of the seat is woven.

With a seat of irregular shape there is a tendency for the strands to bend as they enter some holes. The object is to keep all diagonals as straight and parallel along their lengths as possible and to achieve this, some holes will be 'doubled' – i.e. two of the diagonal strands will have to be pegged into one hole. Corner holes are invariably doubled in this way. Whenever doubling and missing is necessary, it must be done within two or three holes of the corner and within two or three holes of the back end of a short strand. Take care not to let the strand twist as you weave a little of the pattern at a time. If you have worked the pattern correctly, the last diagonal will be very short and go from the holes next to the corner in adjacent rails.

When you have completed the left-hand part of the seat with this diagonal, insert another length of

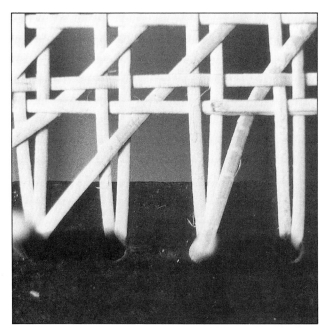

The diagonal on the right is going into the wrong hole. Wherever possible, diagonals should cross under or over the verticals of the front and back rails, and under or over the horizontals of the side rails, before entering a hole.

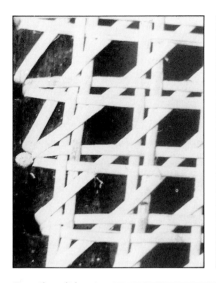

cane into the same corner hole at the back left of the frame, and weave the other half in precisely the same way. Note that if some holes have been doubled on the left rail, the corresponding holes on the right rail will be 'missed' – i.e. no diagonal strands being woven in this step will go into them. These doubles and misses will be worked in the reverse way for *Step 6* – i.e. the *Step 5* doubles will be missed, and the misses will be doubled. If you think you have made a mistake by putting a diagonal into what seems to be an incorrect hole,

Sometimes it is not possible for strands to cross verticals or horizontals before entering holes, so they have to double – two diagonal strands in one hole.

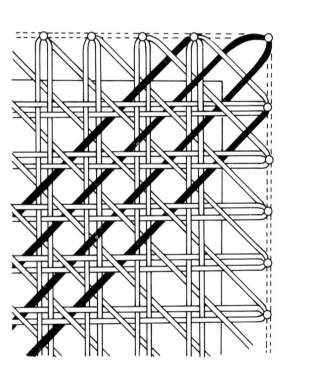

Step 6 (second crossing), over verticals and under horizontals, at right corner of seat.

do not hesitate to take it out. Any error can now be corrected; later on, it may be difficult to do so.

The final step – *Step 6* (*Second Crossing* or *Second Diagonal*) – is woven from the right corner hole at the back to the front corner or left side rail, but reversing the weaving process: instead of weaving over the horizontals and under the verticals, you must go under the horizontals and over the verticals. As already said, doubles and misses are reversed too. The strands are woven at right angles to the diagonals of *Step 5*. Tension will have increased noticeably, and there may be some difficulty in getting the new strand to weave under the existing strands of previous steps before entering or leaving a hole, because the strands will be tight against the wood of the frame. Ease just a little way away from the wood with a bodkin, so that the end of the weaving strand can be slid between cane and frame.

On the side rails, diagonals must end under or over horizontals; on back and front rails, under or over verticals. Exceptions to this occur when holes are doubled, and also those between a double and the nearest corner or the nearest end of a short strand.

Correctly woven, the pattern on the rails will form crosses where *Steps 5* and *6* have gone under or over each other on the rails.

If by some chance you have laid the strands of *Step 3* to the *right* of those of *Step 1*, or have woven the horizontals of *Step 4 below* those of *Step 2* rather than above them, it is of little consequence. In either case, only the weaving of the diagonals is affected. All you must do is make quite sure that the diagonal strands fit snugly into the corners of each of the little squares formed by the first four steps: lying neatly and not rubbing against them, because the friction thus caused would inevitably mean the pattern would not lie correctly and, more important, the seat would quickly fray. The accompanying diagrams and illustrations show how it should appear.

Some caners use the longest possible strands for the diagonals, joining underneath the frame in the usual way. Others cut the diagonal strands to the required length of each diagonal separately. The first method does not require the holes to be pegged, because the long strands give full strength to the weaving. (*See* the section on Pegging, page 83.)

The second method requires each diagonal to be pegged at each end, otherwise the strands may well pull out of the holes. If the individual strands of a seat are not pegged, it can be appreciated that the weight of the body will be almost entirely on the strands of the first four steps (the verticals and horizontals), the diagonals thus doing little more than create the pattern. Sagging of the seat will then be hastened and breaks are likely to occur sooner than they should. For back and side panels, individual strands adequately pegged are sufficient for they do not take so much weight. However, for a strong seat, long strands are advisable.

When using long diagonal strands, try to alternate the loops between holes on the underside as you did with the first four steps.

To finish off the weaving, any lengths of cane hanging beneath the frame must be tied off by twisting round the nearest loop, then cutting off as closely as possible.

One tip on how to weave. Although it is generally easier for one hand to be under the weaving and the other over it, so that the ends of the strands can be fed from one hand to the other, when you come to the last two steps (the diagonals) you can try curving the end of the weaving strand upwards slightly to form a hook. This hook can be threaded between the verticals and horizontals, and saves time.

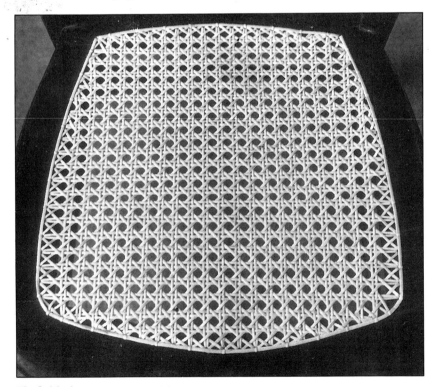

The finished seat.

PEGGING AND BEADING

Before a new seat can be brought back into service, the strands in each hole have to be made firm so that they will not pull out, and if desired the holes in the frame can be covered. These two operations are called pegging and beading.

In genuine antique chairs, the custom was to peg every hole. The fashion for beading – covering the frame holes with wide strips of cane – only came in during the last century.

There are several possible methods of pegging and beading. The most straightforward, of course, is simple pegging, when every frame hole has a peg firmly punched down into it so that the heads are fractionally below the level of the wood. Whenever a peg is inserted into a hole and punched down, care must be taken to see that the surrounding woodwork is not damaged. In former times it was customary for seat weavers to make their own pegs from pieces of wood – a laborious job which fortunately we do not need to do today. We can use round centre cane of a suitable diameter; it cuts easily with a sharp knife, and when tapped in it compresses just enough to ensure a firm hold. If one end is cut at an angle, this facilitates entry into the hole between the strands of cane. The pegs must be long enough to hold the strands, but not so long as to protrude from the holes on the underside of the frame. Never try to force a peg through a strand; the inevitable split in the cane would cause it to weaken.

The most common method of adding beading to the woven pattern is by couching – i.e. by sewing the beading cane into place with lengths of No. 1 or No. 2 seating cane. First, pegs are tapped into alternate holes in each rail or, in the case of frames which are not straight, into alternate holes all the way round the frame. However, if all lengths of cane throughout the weaving have been joined underneath, it is not usually necessary to peg, though many weavers do so nevertheless. With circular and oval frames, the beading is frequently sewn into every hole.

The beading cane used is traditionally one, two or even three sizes wider than the size of cane used for the weaving. The criterion is that it must be wide enough to cover the holes so that they are completely concealed. There are no hard and fast rules governing the size of beading cane: if it looks right, that is all that matters.

If you are going to peg first, select a length of round centre cane which will conveniently go into the holes without having to be banged in hard,

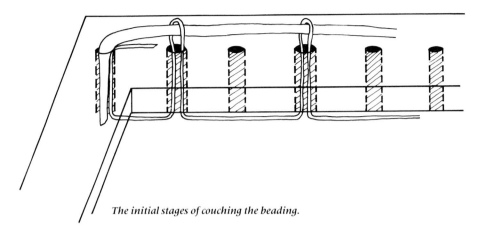

The initial stages of couching the beading.

and cut a sufficient number of pegs. This means that you will first have to work out where the pegs are going, in order to make the beading symmetrically couched. Count from each corner together and work towards the middle of the rail. Tap pegs into the holes next to the back corner holes of the back rail, and others in alternate holes across the rail. Do the same with the front rail and side rails. You may find that in the centre of the rail two pegged or two vacant holes will be adjacent; that is because there is an even number of holes in that rail. With a frame that has curved corners leave every hole on the corners unpegged, to ensure that the beading – when it is couched – follows a smooth curved line.

Both beading and couching canes must be kept damp at all times. Push one end of the couching cane down the first unpegged hole in the back

rail which is nearest the back left corner. Take this end under the frame and up through the corner hole, leaving a couple of inches (c.50mm) protruding. Push one end of the beading cane down into that same corner hole and let the rest of it lie along the back rail; it must be long enough to reach just beyond the opposite corner hole at the back. Hold both the couching cane and the beading cane in the left back corner with a temporary peg.

Now take the long end of the couching cane over the beading cane and back down the hole once more. (You will achieve a smoother finish – particularly on curved parts of a frame – if the couching cane comes up the hole with the glossy side towards the centre of the chair, and goes back down through the outer part of the hole with the glossy side outwards.) Pull the couching cane upwards as it comes out of the hole on the inside of the beading cane, and hold it firmly flat on the underside of the frame with the thumb or forefinger of your other hand; this is one of the operations where one pair of hands is never enough, but you will have to get used to making do with the pair given you! Note that as with the weaving, the glossy side of the cane must always be the side which is visible both on the top and the underside of the frame. Be careful also that the couching cane does not twist underneath the frame as it is travelling between the holes.

Keeping your thumb or forefinger tightly against the couching cane on the underside, with the other hand pull the cane down through the hole so that the beading cane is firmly held in place. Then take the couching cane up through the next unpegged hole, hold it firmly under the frame, bring it over the beading and down through the hole again, keeping both couching and beading canes tight. Continue along the back rail to the other corner. If, as is likely, the holes are already so full of other canes that the couching cane will not go easily into them, ease a way through by carefully inserting the stiletto between the wood and the canes to make a passage large enough for the cane to go through.

At the other end of the back rail, push the beading cane through the corner hole and pull it downwards.

Then push the end of a new length of beading cane down into the same hole (you may have to ease a way for it with the stiletto). Before bending the new length of beading down so that it lies along the side rail, place a peg into the corner hole between the rough underside of the cane and the hole, and tap it in so as to hold both pieces of beading cane. This peg will be concealed when you bring the new length of beading down over it.

The long end of the couching cane is brought across the corner underneath the frame, and up through the first unpegged hole in the right side rail; the couching continues as for the back rail. If it is a straight-edged frame with four clearly defined corner holes, four lengths of beading cane will be required. If the front corners are curved you have left them unpegged for three or four holes, and the system of alternate pegging will not apply. The rule is that every unpegged hole is couched through to hold the beading, except of course the corner holes. Naturally, with such frame shapes you will measure the distance over the holes from the right corner hole at the back all the way round the frame to the left corner hole on the other side, and cut a sufficient length of beading cane to go all round in one piece, with 4in (102mm) or so added on for inserting into the corner holes. Joining of beading cane is possible by couching old and new ends together over the same hole; but it is not advisable, since there is a tendency for a join to work loose or catch in people's clothing. Couching cane can be joined in the same way as in the basic weaving, by knotting or looping beneath the frame.

When the beading cane is all neatly couched in, the end of it has to be threaded down into the corner hole at the back from where it began. It is recommended that the ends of both couching and beading canes are cut to a point so that the beading cane can the more easily be threaded down, and the couching cane threaded up, the same hole. You will need to ease a way through that hole for both canes. When both canes have been firmly

pulled through the hole – the beading cane downwards, the couching cane upwards – they should be held in place by a peg; this peg remains visible, the only one to be seen in this beading process.

Cut off the ends of the beading and couching canes which protrude from the corner holes, close to the frame so that the ends cannot be seen.

If you wish, every hole can be pegged and beading can still finish off the work. In this method, every alternate hole is pegged as before, and the beading cane inserted into the left back corner hole. But no couching cane is needed; instead, the beading cane (which in this case must be narrower than the diameter of the holes) is cut into short lengths. Each

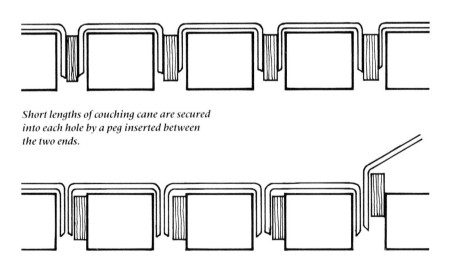

Short lengths of couching cane are secured into each hole by a peg inserted between the two ends.

The peg is inserted between the new end of couching cane and the interior of the hole.

must be long enough to go from one unpegged hole to the next, with a little extra allowed to insert into each unpegged hole. When in the holes, the beading cane should not be so long as to protrude beneath the frame.

Starting from a corner hole, each short length is placed into the next unpegged hole, then another short length is placed in that hole next to it. A peg is tapped into the hole between the two lengths of cane to hold them (and the weaving cane already in that hole) quite firmly. This continues all the way to the next corner – or, in the case of frames with curved corners, right round the frame, using every unpegged hole.

This same technique of pegging the beading can also be done in a way which conceals the heads of the pegs. You will still require short lengths of beading cane, but instead of placing the pegs to hold them *between* the two beading lengths in each hole, they are inserted against the new length so that when it is laid into the next unpegged hole it hides the peg.

Of course, for these two beading methods you will need pegs of smaller diameter than those which you would use to hold only the weaving strands.

Trim off any pieces of beading and couching cane which protrude.

The beading for 'blind' caning (by which each woven strand has to be cut to length to fit the frame holes which have not been drilled right through the wood) can be pegged by either of the last two methods, or it can be given the appearance of having been couched.

The technique of couching in blind holes should not be used for frames with holes drilled right through the frame. In blind hole beading, the cane is pegged into a corner hole in the usual way; the length of beading must be sufficient to extend right across the rail to the extreme corner holes, as in the first method described. It is the *couching* cane which in this method has to be cut into short lengths, measuring twice the depth of each hole. Dampened, the short couching cane lengths are bent into a U-shape, the base being as wide as the beading cane. A small touch of glue squirted into each hole will help to hold all strands of cane, particularly if you are couching into every hole. Normally you will have pegged alternate holes first – or rather, as this is blind hole beading, removed alternate pegs. With each unpegged hole containing a dab of glue, the short bent lengths of couching cane are placed into each hole with the arms of the 'U' going either side of the beading cane, and pressed firmly home.

Note that blind caning is never used for seats: pressure on the cane seating would inevitably pull the canes out of the holes no matter how firmly they might have been glued and pegged.

The same effect of couched beading can be achieved without glue but with pegs and patience. Short sections of couching cane are again prepared as above. These are inserted into each hole over the beading, and held in place by two small-diameter pegs. The latter are often made from matchsticks which can be broken off at the right length more easily than a piece of centre cane. The matchstick pegs are tapped into the hole on each side of the couching cane to hold the beading firm and flat.

In the double-caning method of weaving, where the panel is woven on both sides of the frame, the beading is usually incorporated into the weaving process and not added separately.

The seat is woven, the beading added. Now only one bit of tidying needs to be done before the seat can be said to be ready for use. Depending on the age and quality of the cane you have used, there may be a few hair-fine threads of cane visible which have been stripped off the non-glossy underside during the weaving. These hairs have to be removed to improve the appearance of the finished work. If there are only a few of them they can be cut off individually, close to the strand, without damaging it. However, if that would take too long to do, they can be very carefully singed off. An ordinary butane cigarette lighter is useful for the purpose. Do not hold the flame in one place for too long, otherwise the cane will go up in flames. Keep it moving over the underside and the top of the weave until the hairs have been singed off. Never use a candle, as the deposit of soot will be even more difficult to remove.

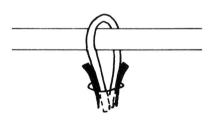

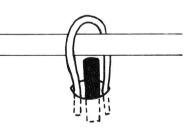

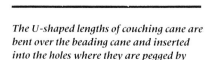

The U-shaped lengths of couching cane are bent over the beading cane and inserted into the holes where they are pegged by

(left) a peg placed between the two legs, or (right) two small pegs either side of the legs.

'BLIND' CANING

A good way to discover if the caning of a back or side panel (never a seat) may have been carried out in this way is to look at the back. There will be no cane visible coming out through the holes and looping into adjoining ones, because the frame holes will not have been drilled all the way through but only to an indeterminate depth. 'Blind' caning is also known as 'French' or 'continental' caning.

There will be times when you come across what is effectively blind caning on an ordinary seat frame. These partially-drilled holes are found usually in chairs in which the caning has been woven before the chair was finally assembled. They are at the corners of the seat frame, above the front legs where these block the exit of the strands underneath the frame, or at the back where the seat frame joins the back uprights. In the weaving process, they must be regarded as blind holes.

Any of the recognized caning patterns can be used in blind caning, although usually it is the six-way standard. Because the holes are only partially drilled into the frame, each strand of cane has to be cut to length and held in place at both ends by pegs during the remainder of the weaving. You will find it preferable to weave with long strands, cutting to length once one strand end is in place, rather than to measure each length before you start to weave it.

Clearing the holes of old cane and pegs in preparation for the weaving of the new panel can be a bit of a problem. Every little piece of old cane and peg must be removed from each hole before the work can start, and this may call for the use of a drill with a depth gauge, particularly if the dirt of years has impacted them.

There is a method of pegging in which each strand is held in place by its own short length of peg, about 1/8in (3mm) long. The strands have to be inserted right into the holes so that they touch bottom. Subsequent canes entering the hole are similarly inserted with their own small piece of peg, without the previous pegs having to be removed. This is an acceptable system for holes which are deeply drilled to something like 1¼in (32mm), but it is a fiddly way of doing it. The more common method is to use pegs which are no longer than the depths of the holes, and to remove them each time a strand is inserted, the peg then being replaced. By the time you get to the next step and the pegs have to be withdrawn, you will find that the strands of the previous step have positioned themselves satisfactorily and are unlikely to be pulled out with the peg. Obviously, with this pegging method there will be pegs in every hole by the time the work is finished.

To weave the six-way standard pattern, insert two strands side by side in the middle hole at the top of the frame, and peg firmly. The other ends of the strands are taken through the corresponding centre hole at the bottom, and again securely pegged. Thus you are laying *Steps 1* and *3* together. Do this on each side of the first pair of verticals until they are all in position. If the panel frame is shaped, you will need to leave holes between the verticals as required in order to keep the pairs parallel and equidistant. Do not pull them too tight or else they may be pulled out of their holes by the subsequent weaving steps.

Steps 2 and *4* are also worked together. Place two canes side by side in the bottom hole of either side, and peg. Weave them alternately to their corresponding hole opposite, and again peg firmly. Carry on weaving these horizontals up to the top of the frame, missing holes wherever necessary. Weaving the horizontals together holds all four canes in place more securely.

Steps 5 and *6* – the diagonals – are woven in the normal way, following the accepted rules for misses and doubles.

Beading is not usual in blind caning, the holes simply being pegged. However, if you should decide to add it, see the section on Pegging and Beading on page 83.

Although at first sight the back of a chair may appear to indicate that the weaving has been done with the blind caning method (because no strands are visible at the back) this may not always be so. The backs of some chairs are caned in the normal way, but the loops which would otherwise be exposed lie in a continuous groove which, when the weaving is complete, has a fillet of wood inserted to conceal the cane loops. The fillet is then sanded down and colour-matched so that the back of the frame appears to be flat and all of one piece. It can be extremely difficult to remove this fillet; it usually fragments as it is being removed, due to age and possibly because glue was originally placed between the cane loops and the underside of the fillet. It is not a simple job to make a new fillet, so unless you have facilities for removing the old one and replacing it, it would be as well to consider this type of frame as one which is most suitable for blind caning.

DOUBLE CANING

In this technique, as the name suggests, two panels of canework are woven separately or simultaneously, on the outside as well as on the inside of a frame. Double caning is found on the backs and arms of armchairs and settees.

It may be that the holes are not drilled right the way through the frame, in which case they are blind holes; the weaving technique for each side is the same, and is described in the section on Blind Caning on page 89.

If the holes are drilled all the way through the frame, the simple way of caning is to do the inside of the frame as if it is a conventional seat frame, while the outside is blind caned. Whichever of these methods you use, each side of the panel has to be caned separately.

There is a third method which, though apparently more complicated, nevertheless gives a stronger finish and is traditionally more authentic.

For each of the three methods an additional tool is required. If you can visualize a double caned panel, you will appreciate that whereas it is a simple matter to cane one side conventionally, it is impossible to use the same technique for the other: with one woven panel in place, the thickness of the frame being no more than a couple of inches (51mm), it is not possible to get your hand between it and the other panel in order to feed the strands through from the back to the front of the weaving. To facilitate this part of the work I use an ordinary teaspoon with a bent undecorated handle, which can be inserted between the woven strands so that the end of the new strand can be guided by it. Any old teaspoon will do, provided that the handle is smooth. Or a small cup hook screwed into a holder can hook the new strands between the weaving.

Steps 1 to *4* are first worked in their normal sequence on the inside of the panel, the strands alternating on the outer side so that loops are created between every hole. Then the same steps are worked on the outside in the same way – using the teaspoon handle to guide the *Step 4* strands through between those of *Steps 1* and *3*. The loops made between the holes on both sides of the panel do service as beading.

The strands of the diagonals of *Steps 5* and *6* are worked together on opposite sides. Each strand is passed through the appropriate hole in the top of the panel so that there is enough length on either side for it to be woven, going through the side rail and woven back down on the opposite side to the bottom rail, where it is pulled through and pegged. An extra inch or two (up to 50mm) of cane is left to protrude from the bottom hole for final tensioning.

To obtain identical patterns on the outside and inside of the panel, the shorter diagonals of *Step 5* and *6* should in the same holes on each side. This will in turn mean that the misses and doubles on each side will also coincide.

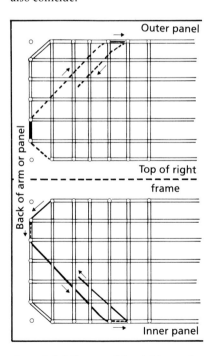

An exploded diagram of the right arm of a double caned chair, showing the direction of the weaving cane in the working of the two diagonals of Steps 5 and 6 simultaneously.

The diagram shows both outer and inner sides of a panel, which for clarity is assumed to have corners which are at right angles.

A strand is threaded through the hole on the top of the panel which is next to the corner hole, with enough of it hanging down on each side to be woven diagonally to the bottom via the side rail, or upright. Thread the inner length of cane through the hole below the top corner hole in the upright rail. It comes out on the outside of the panel, from whence it is woven in the normal way as a diagonal on the outside, until it comes to the bottom of the panel. There it is threaded into the appropriate outside hole and through to the inside, where it is pegged with an inch or two (25–50mm) protruding.

The other end of the same strand is still hanging on the outside of the panel. Thread it through the same hole on the side rail as the other end has gone through, but in the opposite direction, and weave it down on the inside of the panel to the bottom. Here it goes through the already-threaded hole and out to hang for an inch or two (25–50mm) after being securely pegged. Make sure that none of the pegs is so long as to push out those on the other side of the panel which are in the same hole.

That is the way to weave a diagonal on both sides of the panel using one strand, and the sequence continues over the frame: succeeding strands are passed through the next holes in line at the top of the panel, one end is woven diagonally through to the upright (or the bottom rail, when all the holes in the upright are used up), then threaded through to continue being woven to the next rail, where it is pegged into its hole before the other end of the strand is woven identically on the other face of the panel. The sequence continues until every hole in the top of the panel has a diagonal in it. Pegging in every hole as the strands go through, not only the ends of strands, is recommended.

Then, starting from the top back corner of the frame, repeat the whole process over again in the opposite direction.

The diagonal strands which are woven into doubled holes are all started in the hole at the other end of the diagonal. The strand is woven diagonally from the top rail, taken through the doubled hole in the upright rail, and woven on the other side of the panel before being pegged into its starting hole. The diagonal which partners it into the same doubled hole starts in the next hole in the top rail, weaves down into the same doubled hole, through it, and up to finish in its starting hole, where it is pegged.

When all the diagonals have been woven, remove each peg one by one, pulling tight the end of cane protruding; replace the peg to hold the cane secure, then cut off the excess length as close as possible to it.

Additional beading is not usual in this double caning method, but if it is required the methods are as described for blind caning.

BOW-FRONTED FRAMES

There are numerous variations in seat frame shapes, and it would be impossible to give instructions for the weaving of each. None has enormous difficulties; all can be adapted from the instructions given for square and round frames.

The most common variations are those seats with bow fronts, and a few remarks concerning these may be helpful.

In general, the pairs of verticals and horizontals (*Steps 1* to *4*) should be kept as far as possible equidistant and parallel. This will necessitate missing one or two holes between the last few weavings of *Steps 1* and *3* at the sides, and *Steps 2* and *4* at the front. Holes along the front of the frame must always have in them the weavings of *Steps 1* and *3*. In fact, the only holes without vertical and/or horizontal

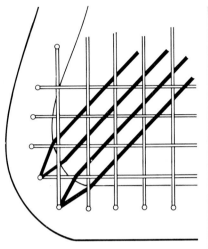

Nominating a corner hole.

strands are those at the two back corners.

Front 'corner' holes are nominated as those where the shortest strands of *Steps 1* and *3* reach the front of the frame, even though the strands of each of the first four steps will probably be already in them. The hole immediately above a front corner hole is doubled, as is the corner hole itself.

For instructions on the beading of the front corner curves, see the section on Pegging and Beading on page 83.

ROUND AND OVAL FRAMES

The technique for the six-way standard method of weaving a round or oval frame is precisely the same as for a straight-edged seat, although the sequence of steps can be varied. The method here described is applicable to both shapes.

One thing which it is particularly important to get right is the symmetry of *Steps 1* and *2*. Ideally, there should be an even number of holes equally spaced round the edge of the frame and divisible by four, so that the two sides and the top and bottom of the pattern are identical. On this point, beware of drop-in seats – those which can be lifted out of the seat frame, though frequently held in place by screws. You must mark the

exact front of the frame before you remove it, or else your pattern could be woven off-centre.

These frame holes are not always exact: either there is an odd number of holes, or they are not equally spaced – or both. But this should not be too much of a problem. Count the number of holes on each side of the middle hole at the back, and mark those three holes in the frame which are spaced one quarter, one half, and three-quarters of the way round – that is, at 90°, 180° and 270°.

In a frame where the number of holes is divisible by four, there will be the same number of holes between the marks. If there is an odd number of holes, or they are not equally spaced, mark those which are as near as possible to the four quarter-points, so as to make the intersections of the verticals and horizontals as near-perfect right angles as possible.

Start *Step 1* by pegging one end of your cane into the middle hole at the back, and take the other end down through the corresponding hole at the front. Bring it up through the adjacent hole to the left, across to the back, and down the next hole, and so on. As your strands get closer to the side of the pattern, you will have to miss some holes in the frame in order to keep the verticals as equidistant and as parallel as possible. Then weave the right half of the frame.

For *Step 2*, peg the end of a strand into the 270° marked hole on the left, take it over the strands and across to the 90° marked hole on the right. Continue laying the strands horizontally until you get close to the top and bottom, when (as with *Step 1*) you will have to miss a hole here and there so that they are also equidistant and parallel. Try to miss the same

Steps 1 and 2 in place. Because of the regularity in the positioning of the holes, it is often impossible to keep the shorter strands equidistant. So long as they are parallel, this will make little difference to the appearance of the finished pattern.

The first diagonal has been woven. Note where the doubles are.

The second vertical lies to the side of the first and over both previous steps.

holes symmetrically as those you missed during the laying of *Step 1*, although this will not always be possible; keeping them equidistant and parallel is the prime consideration.

The sequence of steps can now be changed from the usual *Steps 3, 4, 5* and *6* of the six-way-pattern. Indeed, some professional seat weavers use this alternative sequence in all their six-way caning. If you wish to continue with *Steps 1* to *6* as on a straight frame, there is no reason why you should not do so, but I find it better to make the next step the first diagonal weave. By this means (making what was *Step 5* become *Step 3*) the strands of the first two steps are held more firmly in position. You will find this sequence particularly useful if you should be weaving the back of a chair which curves in one sweep and has a curved top.

For this step (the first diagonal) start from the left front corner hole and take the strand to the right rear corner hole, going under the verticals and over the horizontals of *Steps 1* and 2. How (you may well ask) do you find a corner hole in a round or oval frame? A good question. The answer is that you have to nominate one – not arbitrarily, but with some degree of precision. Take the top left arc of the frame (the north-west segment, as it were); mark the hole that is below and next to the shortest vertical strand, and mark also the hole above and next to the shortest horizontal strand. The middle hole (or holes) which lie between these two marks can be regarded as the centre hole(s), and should have doubles in them as in straight-framed corner holes. Ignore the fact that in round and oval frames you are doubling in corner holes which already have other strands in them.

Do the same at each of the other three points of the compass – NE, SE, and SW – to find their corner holes.

So the first diagonal (whether you are following the customary or the alternative sequence of steps) goes from a corner hole in the south-west to a corner hole in the north-east. Continue weaving until this step has

been completed, missing and doubling as necessary and if possible using the same holes in the corresponding segments of the frame. You will find that all the misses and doubles will occur relatively close together in the segments. They do not occur in the middle of the back, front, or sides.

The next step in this alternative sequence is the second vertical and is laid (not woven) over the strands already in place and to the side of the first vertical.

The second horizontal is the next step, and is woven from the right of the frame, over and under the two verticals of each pair – but also under the diagonal. Begin at the back of the frame and weave each strand above the first horizontal strands. If you suspect that by the time you get the weaving down to the front of the frame the tension may be so taut that

The second horizontal is woven between each vertical pair and under the diagonal.

you might have difficulty in weaving at the front (particularly if the horizontal strands lie across the wood of the frame), it is permissible to weave the short horizontals at the front first. If you do this, remember to weave *above* the short strands.

Step 6 (unchanged in sequence) is the second diagonal and is woven from the right front corner (the south-east) under the horizontals and over the verticals, and alternating over and under the first diagonal. Both diagonals must lie smoothly between the crossings of each pair of verticals and horizontals in order to avoid snagging.

Pegging and beading are carried out in the way described earlier. However, with round and oval

frames it is frequently the case that the beading is either omitted or the couching cane is sewn through every hole and not just through alternate ones. This is because of the continuous curve of the frame. Couching in alternate holes of round and oval frames does not allow the beading to bend sideways satisfactorily enough to lie in a smooth and flat curve. If couching has to be in every hole, then of course there is no way in which the strands can be firmly pegged in their holes; therefore it is important that each step of the weaving should be worked with long strands, joined underneath in the usual way, so that there can be no chance of any of the ends slipping out.

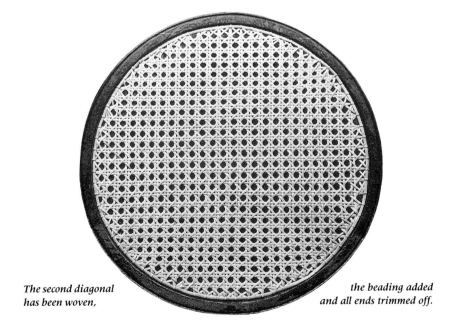

The second diagonal has been woven,

the beading added and all ends trimmed off.

BOWED CHAIR BACKS

Should you have the opportunity to re-cane an armchair which has a bowed sloping back, think twice before passing it up because you think it will be too difficult. Bergère, corner and tub chairs of past days are delightful pieces which can grace any home. Their intricate canework wraps round back and arms in one graceful sweep in frame shapes which can be a combination of curves, straights and bows. Although it may seem a formidable project to attempt, it is all based on the traditional six-way method of weaving. Certainly it calls for considerable practice in the less complex shapes of frame, but it will be well worth the time, effort and concentration spent on it.

To restore the canework to its original glory it is virtually essential to make an accurate sketch of the old work before you remove it, as there can be variations in the basic method.

Mark the middle hole at the top of the back and at the bottom; if there are an even number of holes in either top or bottom, or the two middle ones do not give an accurate vertical alignment, mark whichever is nearest to the middle and be prepared to adjust the later stages of the weaving to make the pattern appear to match on both sides of the frame. Weave *Step 1* vertically, starting from the bottom marked hole. The strands of this step delineate the shape of the curve. There are two points to note.

First: some of these chairs also have a caned seat, and the holes at the back of the seat frame serve also as the holes for the bottom of the back. If the seat is intact and does not require re-weaving, take special care when you remove the pegs and the old back cane so that you disturb as little as possible of the seat caning.

Second: possibly there may be more holes in the top edge of the back frame than there are in the bottom of it; in which case refer to your sketch to ascertain precisely where each of the verticals goes. Every bottom hole should have a vertical coming up from it, but because of the shape of the back and sides it may be necessary to miss holes in the top of the frame to ensure that the *Step 1* strands are vertical all the way round. Alternatively, as they approach the arm supports the verticals may not be truly vertical but slope towards the back of the chair. In this variation of the pattern, the top front corners of each arm may need to be filled in with short additional strands of 'verticals' woven from the arm supports to the spare holes in the top.

The horizontal strands of *Step 2* are laid *behind* the verticals of *Step 1* with just sufficient tension to keep them approximately horizontal without pulling the verticals forward. Weave *Step 2* from the bottom hole in the left arm support. The nearer the weaving gets to the top of the frame, so holes will have to be missed and doubled in order to maintain the parallels of the horizontals.

To hold these first two steps in place, the next step to be woven is the first diagonal. Starting from the corner hole at the junction of the left arm support and the seat frame, weave diagonally towards the top of the back, going under the horizontals and over the verticals, missing and doubling in suitable holes to maintain the gentle curving of the diagonal strands. The strands of both diagonals are not to be woven with long lengths of cane, but should be cut to length.

The second verticals are positioned next. These are placed (not woven) behind the strands of the previous three steps, and use the same holes as the first verticals. They must, of course, lie to the right of *Step 1* strands as they come through the holes to the front. As the back of the chair is visible, it is important to bring the strands of each vertical out at the back and through adjacent holes so that there is a continuous run of loops between the holes, and that each is pegged.

The second horizontal is woven from the opposite front button

corner, over the diagonal, under the first vertical and over the second of each pair. If the strands of the first horizontal have become slack with the weaving of the diagonal, re-tension them from the bottom in the direction in which they were woven.

Finally weave the second diagonal, doubling and missing to balance the misses and doubles of the first, and going under the verticals and over the horizontals.

Because of the continuous curve of the back of the frame, beading would be unlikely to lie flat even if every hole were to be couched. Also, because the diagonals have been cut to length, it is therefore customary to finish off by pegging every hole.

Sometimes the horizontals of *Step 2*, as they near the top of the back, follow the curve of the frame instead of being woven parallel to each other (check your sketch of the original work). For this variation, *Steps 1* and *3* must be worked together before *Steps 2* and *4* are woven. *Steps 2* and *4* are also woven together, from opposite arm supports. They must not be pulled so tight in the weaving as to draw the verticals forward. As the weaving nears the top and begins to follow the line of the curve of the frame, *Steps 2* and *4* will tend to hold each other in position. The diagonals are woven normally, after which the horizontals will almost certainly need to be re-tensioned.

SADDLEBACKS

The majority of caned seats and panels are flat – in other words, all four sides of the frame are on the same plane. However, from time to time one comes across a piece of caned furniture with a concave frame: the seats and backs of folding chairs and bedroom stools are the most common. I call these 'saddleback frames'.

There are three convenient ways of caning such frames, but the first two methods described are more time-consuming than the third.

One method is to work the first step between the curved (usually

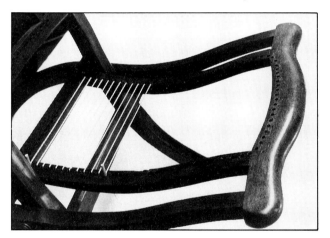

The first step is worked from side to side across the frame to delineate the curve.

The longer strands of Step 2 lie beneath those of Step 1 without distorting the curve of the latter.

side) rails, instead of from rear to front, in order to determine the curved shape of the seat. The second step is laid in the usual way, except that the strands go *beneath* those of the first step, so that they too follow the curve of the frame. They must lie lightly against the underside of the strands of *Step 1;* tension them too firmly and the curve will be pulled out of shape. *Step 3* is laid beneath the first two steps, again lightly and without excess tension. The strands of *Step 3* will of course lie to one side of the *Step 1* strands as they come up out of the holes. *Step 4* is woven in the customary method, followed by *Steps 5* and *6* (the diagonals.)

The second method is to work *Step 1* as above, and *Step 3* at the same time, starting from the opposite side of the frame. Both steps are worked together. *Step 2* is next, and has to be woven under and over the strands of *Steps 1* and *3. Step 4* is woven in the opposite sequence; *Steps 5* and *6* are woven normally.

The third method – which I find to be the quickest – is to work *Steps 1* and *3* first, as in the previous instructions. Before working the next step (*Step 2*), however, get a smooth, narrow strap of plastic or leather; this should be a few inches longer than twice the distance between the holes of the other two rails through which *Steps 2* and *4* will be woven. In the middle of this strap bore a small hole, just large enough to take a piece of your weaving cane, whatever size it

In the second method, Steps 1 and 3 are worked together from alternate sides in order to create the correct sequence of loops on the underside.

The thin leather strap has been woven between Steps 1 and 3. An end of a strand has been inserted into a hole in the strap ready to be pulled through to the opposite rail.

may be. Weave this strap under and over the two strands of the steps you have already laid, and leave the hole in it outside one of the rails. Push the end of your weaving strand through this hole for an inch or so, and bend it back on itself. Now pull the strap through until the hole in the strap – with the strand in it – is at the opposite rail. Remove the strand from the strap, take it down into the appropriate frame hole and up through the next one; insert it into the hole in the strap and pull the strap back to the other rail, where the strand is threaded through the frame hole and up the next one and into the strap again. Continue right across the frame in this way, being careful not to pull the strands so tightly as to distort

the curved shape. Of course, the strap should be removed when *Step 2* is complete.

Do make sure that the strap you use is really smooth: any sharp edges or bits sticking out could snag the strands of *Steps 1* and *3* as you are pulling it through.

Step 4 of this method is woven under and over the strands of *Steps 1* and *3*, as in the six-way; similarly the diagonals of *Steps 5* and *6*. You may find it advantageous to work the diagonals of *Steps 5* and *6* together. Weave a diagonal strand in one direction first, then weave the corresponding diagonal in the other direction; and so on across the seat. This sequence helps to define the finished concave shape more easily.

DOUBLE SADDLEBACKS

A variation on the ordinary saddleback might best be described as the double saddleback. More often than not, this is found on the back of a chair: the vertical side rails of the frame form a flattened 'S' shape, while the horizontal top and bottom bars are also slightly curved.

To weave this satisfactorily without distorting the whole of the canework, string four or five vertical strands equally spaced from the top to the bottom bars in order to delineate the curve. These strands are only temporary and will be removed as the weaving progresses.

Step 1 involves setting horizontal strands behind these temporary ones. Do not over-tension them; let them lie firmly at the back of the temporary strands but not so tight as to pull the latter out of shape.

Temporary strands in place.

The horizontal strands are laid behind the temporary ones to delineate the curve of the frame.

In *Step 2*, the verticals are laid behind those of *Step 1* – again, just tightly enough. The temporary vertical strands are removed as the work progresses, when the strands of *Step 2* need to go through these holes.

Step 3 – lay these horizontally behind the strands of *Steps 1* and *2*.

Step 4 is woven normally; *Steps 5* and *6* can be worked together (alternating the direction of each strand) to ensure the double curve is maintained.

Because of the curves, it is unusual for this particular method to be finished off with beading. However, the normal beading methods can be followed if required.

OTHER PATTERNS

It is perfectly sensible to wonder if, as there is a six-way standard pattern, there is also a five-way standard. There is; and a four-way; and one or two others, all with variations. None is as strong as the six-way standard, but all look attractive. If they are used for seat weaving, they should be treated with care and regarded as more decorative than functional.

These patterns are best suited to square and rectangular frames. Most of them can be easily adapted for shaped frames, but the pattern then tends to become distorted at the edges. Whereas the six-way standard pattern is governed by the holes, in some of the others the aim is to achieve symmetry no matter where the holes in the frame are situated.

In the five-way and four-way patterns, the diagonals should cross each other on the horizontals and verticals as illustrated. The diagonals of the Single and Double Victoria patterns cross in the centre of the squares formed by the horizontals and verticals.

Beading can be added in most of these other patterns, using any of the methods already described in the

Five-way standard pattern.

section on Pegging and Beading (*see* page 83).

FIVE-WAY STANDARD

For the five-way standard pattern, two verticals of No. 2 cane are placed side by side in every hole in the front and back rails. This is followed by a single strand of No. 2 cane woven horizontally from a side rail, over and under the alternate double strands (treated as one strand). The two diagonals, which may be of No. 2 or No. 3 cane, are woven singly as in the six-way standard.

Alternatively, two verticals are placed side by side from each hole as in the previous method. But here the single horizontal weavings change: the first is woven over the first strand of each vertical pair, and under the second, across the frame; through the hole in the opposite rail and up the next one, from where it is woven alternately under and over the individual strands of the verticals back across the frame. The third row of horizontal weaving repeats the sequence of the first row; the fourth repeats the second; and so on to the back of the frame. The diagonals are woven in No. 3 cane in the usual way.

Five-way alternative pattern.

FOUR-WAY STANDARD

The basic four-way standard pattern looks more attractive if it is woven with No. 4 cane for the verticals and horizontals, and No. 2 or 3 for the diagonals, although the same size of cane – usually either No. 2 or No. 3 – can be worked throughout. There is only a single strand used for each step: one vertical, one horizontal and two diagonals. The first two steps are laid in the usual way, with the horizontals lying over the verticals, not woven. The diagonals are woven under the verticals and over the horizontals.

In this and the following two patterns, the corner holes must not be doubled, only one diagonal strand being threaded through each of them.

Four-way standard pattern.

SINGLE VICTORIA

A third variation of the four-way pattern is better known as the Single Victoria. It takes little time to work and is definitely more decorative than functional, lacking considerably in strength in common with other four-way methods.

Each step is worked with a single strand. The horizontals are laid over the verticals, and the first diagonal is laid over the verticals, and the first diagonal is laid over the previous two steps so that the strands lie precisely on top of the crossings. The second diagonal is the only step that is woven; it goes over the first diagonal and under the crossings of the verticals and horizontals. In this pattern, only single strands are threaded into the corner holes, not doubles.

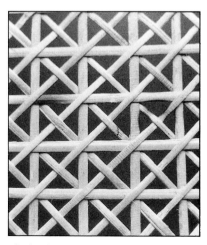

Single Victoria pattern.

DOUBLE VICTORIA

The Double Victoria pattern is in essence identical to the Single Victoria, except that the strands of each step may be doubled. Two No. 2 strands of verticals are laid side by side from each hole across the frame. Similarly, two strands of No. 3 cane are laid over them horizontally from the side rail holes. The first diagonal is laid in No. 4 cane from a back corner hole diagonally over the crossings of the verticals and horizontals; only one diagonal strand is placed in each corner hole. The second diagonal, also using No. 4 cane, is woven from the opposite back corner hole over the first diagonals and under the crossings.

Variations on the Double Victoria have their own charm. The first involves using double strands of No. 2 cane for each of the first three steps – vertical, horizontal, and first diagonal. For the final step (the second diagonal) No. 3 cane is woven over the first diagonal and under the crossings of the first two steps.

The second minor variation is to use two strands of No. 2 cane lying side by side for the final diagonal step.

Double Victoria pattern.

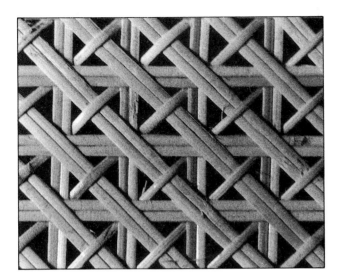

Double Victoria pattern, first variation.

Double Victoria pattern, second variation.

If the frame holes are close together, this variation gives the effect of the weaving having been close-caned.

SPIDER'S WEB

Spider's Web is a caning pattern used only in the back panels of large chairs. It is a good name for the method, which has a block or medallion (the 'spider') in the centre of the frame with the strands encircling and radiating from it like the rays of the sun – hence its alternative name of Sun Ray. Occasionally the block will be oval in shape, but the method of weaving is virtually the same.

As with other difficult projects – and I would emphasize that this pattern is not for anyone who has not

mastered the six-way standard – it is advisable first to make an accurate sketch of the pattern, noting into which holes the strands of cane go, where the doubles and misses occur, what form the encircling strands take and so on.

In making your sketch, one of the most important points is which way up the block should be, particularly if it has a carved or painted decoration. The first stage in the weaving of the new panel, even before cutting the old canework, is to position the block centrally in the frame. There are three possible ways of doing this:

The broken Spider's Web pictured here has the pattern in concentric circles. There is enough of the old cane still in place to allow an accurate sketch of the pattern to be made.

This chair back has the Spider's Web woven as a spiral, starting from the bottom left segment of the central block and finishing left of centre at the bottom of the frame.

1 Tie it in place with fine string threaded through four equidistant holes in the block and into corresponding holes in the frame. This means that some adjustment will have to be made during the initial stages of the work to ensure that it remains absolutely central.

2 Clamp it to a length of wood which itself is clamped to the top and bottom of the frame, slightly off-centre.

3 Place two small nails in the top and bottom of the frame through holes which are slightly off-centre, having first carefully removed the old cane and pegs from them; the nails must not be a tight fit, but should move easily in them so that they can be fixed into a wooden slat long enough to extend diagonally a little beyond the outer edges of the top and bottom of the frame. The old canework may be loose, so position the block centrally and then place two more nails through suitable holes in it to be nailed into the slat.

If the holes in the block or the frame are blind, clamping the block into position is the only effective way of centralizing it. If the old canework has already been removed, then the only method of centralizing the block is by first taking careful measurement.

Now you can cut away the old cane, close to the inner edges of the frame and the block. Clear the pegs from all holes by gently punching them through from the back. You will see that the holes in the block are much smaller than those in the frame, and these must be cleared with extreme care – I punch them out with a small nail, having blunted the point – because the block holes are very close together and undue forcing could result in the wood splitting. If gentle punching through does not clear them, they will need to be drilled out.

Should the holes be blind, this need present no problems in the caning (*see*

In the chair illustrated, the slat was fixed to the front of the frame and nailed to the back of the block, in existing nail holes, because the frame was curved. Tension would have been wrong if the slat had been fixed to the back of the frame as well. There was enough of the old cane left in place for the block to remain perfectly centralized, so the slat was fixed before the old cane was cut away.

section on Blind Caning on page 89), but it may not be easy to remove every particle of peg and old cane without drilling.

Though at first sight it may not seem to be so, the method of caning is that of the six-way standard, with two verticals interwoven with two horizontals, and two diagonals in opposite directions. Perhaps it may help you to visualize the similarity of method if you regard the central block as the front rail of a normal seat frame, with the back and sides varying according to the area of the pattern being woven.

The sizes of cane usually used are Nos. 1 and 2, or Nos. 2 and 3. As the holes in the block are considerably smaller and closer together than those in the frame, they cannot take the same sizes of cane which can fit into the larger frame holes. Similarly, pegs for the block holes are necessarily smaller in diameter than those in the frame: often they are so small that the most suitable pegs are matchsticks, which can be broken off when the weaving has been completed.

The strands of the first step – in effect, the verticals – are laid in four different parts of the pattern first; this is to take the strain of the block and to hold it correctly once the supports have been removed. Firmly peg a length of the smaller size of cane into the top left corner hole of the frame,

leaving 1in (25mm) or so protruding from the back. Thread the other end through the corresponding hole in the left quadrant of the block. Peg the strand firmly in the block before threading it through the next block hole above, where it is pegged and left hanging for the time being.

The second strand is pegged into the opposite corner hole in the frame at the bottom right. If there is no obvious corner hole (as in the case of a circular or oval frame), place the strand in the hole which is diagonally in line with the first strand you have positioned, leaving a short length hanging from the peg after you have pegged firmly. Thread the weaving end through the hole in the block which corresponds to the second frame hole; then bring it through the adjoining hole below it, and peg. There should be the same number of unused holes in both block and frame in the two halves of the frame.

A third strand is inserted into the top right corner hole of the frame and pegged. Then it is threaded through the corresponding hole in the block, pegged, and brought through the next hole below it, and again pegged.

A fourth strand is fixed in the same way on the left of the frame: pegged in the left corner hole which is diametrically opposite the pegged strand in the right corner, threaded through the corresponding hole in the left edge of the block and pegged before being brought out to the front through the next hole above it, and there pegged. Each of the four hanging strands are now pegged into their appropriate frame holes.

The four strands you have pegged in place are anchoring the block centrally; the tension should be equal in each of them, particularly if the block is supported by string. Clamped, or nailed into a slat, the block will still of coure be immovable, and the tension of the strands should be such that it stays in position when the supports are eventually removed. If you have used string supports, check now to verify that the block has not been pulled off-centre. Frequent checking for this should be carried

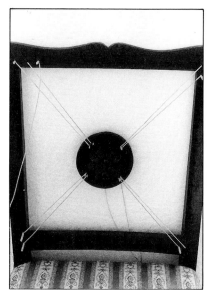

The block suspended from the four corners of this chair back.

out until all the verticals of *Steps 1* and *2* are in place and are taking the strain equally.

Starting with the strand hanging down from the top left of the block, continue threading it through the back rail and block in a clockwise direction until it reaches the next strand a quarter of the way round the pattern. Peg it into the last hole in that quadrant, and cut it off at the back to leave about 2in (51mm) protruding.

Move to the opposite quadrant; starting with the strand hanging from the bottom of the block, thread it through the next hole in the bottom of the frame and so on through to the next strand, pegging every hole as you progress. Cut off this strand at the back and leave 2in (51mm) protruding before taking the next length of strand and threading similarly up to the top of the block and frame, where it is finished off as before.

Finally, weave the strand still hanging from the block, pegging as you go in every hole, but do not cut off the remainder at the back.

While weaving, you will have come to the rigid supports affixed at two points of the block and frame. Of course, before being able to weave through the holes which have been inevitably covered by them, the supports will have had to be removed. After threading the strands through these holes, check the tension of the strands already in place and make sure that the block remains central, before replacing the supports and continuing weaving. Once the first set of *Step 1* verticals is in place, the supports for the block can be removed altogether. Check again that the block is still central; if not, tighten the appropriate strands to make it so and loosen the opposite ones accordingly.

Using the fourth strand end, continue weaving round the frame. It is immaterial in which direction you work this second vertical (clockwise or anticlockwise), so long as the loops at the back of the frame between the holes are alternated. As the back of the chair will be visible, a continuous row of loops will present a tidier appearance than if both vertical strands are looped between the same holes.

For the same reason, it is inadvisable to join strands by knotting at the back. To add a new strand, peg the end firmly into the same hole as the old one, and continue weaving. This method of joining applies only to the strands of *Steps 1* and *3*; those of the subsequent steps are cut to length and are not threaded through adjacent holes to create loops at the back.

As the holes in the block are of small diameter, it may not be possible for the two strands to lie properly side

by side as they come out of them. There will be ample room for them to lie side by side in the frame holes, however, and you should now check to see that they are doing so.

There are two ways of weaving the 'horizontals' of *Steps 2* and *4* so that they encircle the block. One method is to weave concentric circles (or ovals, if it is an oval block). The other way is to weave a continuous spiral, starting from a hole somewhere at the bottom of the block and ending at the hole in the frame which roughly corresponds to it. Check with your sketch which of the two methods was used for the original pattern, and how many concentric circles or spiral weavings there should be. You will probably find that the distances between them increase the nearer they are to the edge of the frame. For

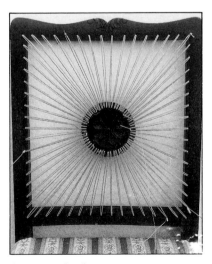

Step 3 completed.

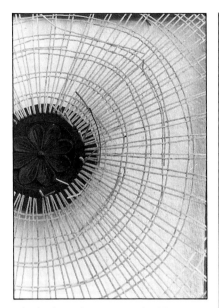

The 'horizontals' are woven in this case as concentric circles. Note that the work at this stage is very loose and still has to be tensioned, starting with the 'horizontal' circles nearest the block. Note also that the joins are staggered, no two of them falling in the same place on the circle.

either method, the 'horizontals' nearest the block should not be too close to it, in order to allow sufficient space for the strands of both diagonals to be eventually woven in.

For the weaving of the 'horizontals' of *Steps 2* and *4* in concentric circles, strands of the smaller of the two sizes of cane you are using are worked in pairs. They do not have their ends pegged into holes in the frame or the block. Begin weaving with one strand under and over the individual strands of *Steps 1* and *3* from any vertical near the block. Weave in a clockwise

direction. When you have woven a sufficient distance for the strand to be held in position, manoeuvre the weave towards the block. Now start weaving the second strand from the same point, but this time over and under the strands. Continue weaving with the first strand all the way round the block to where it started, a few weaves at a time, then weave the second strand for the same distance. Weave a few more times with the first strand, then with the second again, constantly easing both strands towards the block to maintain the circle (or oval), and not allowing any slack.

When they have returned round the block to their starting point, they have to be joined. To do this, weave another three or four times through the verticals so that the tail ends overlap their own front ends. Leave 2in (51mm) of each end of both strands loose before cutting off.

The next pair of strands is worked together in precisely the same way, but do not start these from the same point as the first pair. The start/finish point of each pair of encircling strands should be staggered round the work so that no two joins fall in the same place in the pattern along the verticals. Refer to your sketch to see how many circles of *Steps 2* and *4* there should be, and how far one circle is from the previous one. Near the block they may be as close as ½in

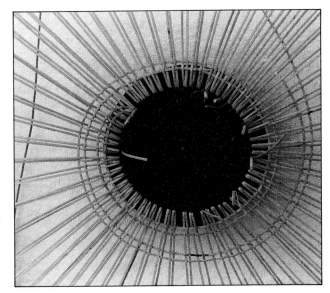

Alternatively, the 'horizontals' can be woven as one continuous spiral. The spiral can start from any hole in the block . . .

(13mm) apart; towards the outside of the pattern, as it nears the edge of the frame, they may be as much as 1½in or 2in (38mm or 51mm) apart.

It is uncommon for the frame itself to be circular or oval; in most cases it is roughly rectangular, with corners which will have to be filled in with two or more short rows of weaving. These must also follow the curve of the concentric circles, and are woven from side holes to holes in the top or bottom of the frame. With circular or oval frames, the 'horizontal' strands will encircle the block parallel to it and the frame, and will not therefore need such short rows.

The above instructions apply equally to oval blocks. However, if the block is set in a frame with corners the strands of *Steps 2* and *4,*

after following the shape of the block for a few weaves away from the centre, occasionally open out into circles as they near the edge of the frame.

The alternative way of weaving the 'horizontals' is in the form of a spiral, using long lengths of the smaller size of cane. From any hole in the edge of the block, two long strands are pegged securely and each in turn is woven once round the block as in the previous method. When they reach their starting point, they continue the weaving, not being cut off but proceeding on the outside of the first round.

This spiral weave continues uninterrupted until both strands reach the hole in the frame which is at the other end of the vertical from which they started. They are then pegged. Joins in this spiral method – if they have to be made – are by overlapping as described above. Gradually, as the spiral grows, the distance between one pair of 'horizontals' and the next should be increased. Short rows of weaving are added to the corners as described.

Weaving of the diagonals (*Steps 5 an 6*) is the same for both circles and spiral methods. Each is woven separately and follows the same procedure as for the six-way standard diagonals. Start *Step 5* by pegging a strand of larger size into a hole in the block; it is not important which hole

is used, though traditionally it is one in the bottom edge. Weave under and over each pair of 'verticals' and 'horizontals', making sure that they nestle snugly into the intersections and do not snag against them. The diagonal will quite naturally curve itself towards the frame. When the strand reaches the frame it is cut off and the end pegged into the appropriate frame hole.

Doubles and misses will occur in the corners of the frame if there are more holes in the frame then in the block. Let your eye be the judge of where these doubles and misses should be.

Before proceeding with the second diagonal (*Step 6*) you will almost certainly find that the first diagonal has slackened the circles (or the spiral, as the case may be) and pulled those strands out of place. You will have to tighten each strand in every circle or all the way along the spiral by carefully taking up the slack and easing them into their correct positions again. If you have woven circles, you will find the excess inches at the end of each strand will help to pull the strands tight once more. Make sure they overlap at each end still.

Now work the second diagonal (*Step 6*) in the normal way, cutting the strands and pegging them at both ends. When the weaving of this diagonal has been completed, you

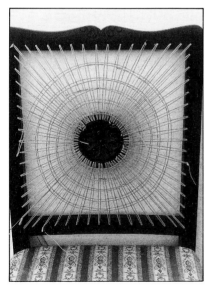

. . . and end at the frame near the 'vertical' from which it started. Here the spiral still has to be tensioned and spaced. Note that joins (which are fewer than in the concentric circle method) are staggered.

The first diagonal is woven outwards from the block, over the 'verticals' and under the 'horizontals', irrespective of whether the latter are concentric circles or a spiral. Note that this particular chair back has square corners, requiring short strands to fill the corners. Re-tensioning is still to be done.

may find it necessary to re-tension the circles or spiral yet again. If so, dampen the strands before tensioning, which will enable them to be positioned more easily than if they are dry.

When you are sure that every strand in the work is correctly tensioned, cut off the spare ends of the overlapping joins in the circles or spiral; do this as close as possible to the last strand each has been woven under, so that the end rests against the back of it. A dab of transparent

adhesive on the overlaps at the back of the pattern could help to secure them, though if the tensions are correct this should not be necessary.

Because of the smallness and closeness of the holes in the block, it is not possible to add beading. Sometimes beading is added to the frame, but this is unusual: the distances between holes in the top two corners of the frame are so great as to prevent beading from lying flat. Therefore all strands, in block and frame holes, are held steady by pegs which are tapped firmly into the frame, and the matchstick pegs in the block are broken off before excess cane ends are trimmed.

Your panel may have a block which is square or rectangular and is set in a rectangular frame. Neither of the two methods described is suitable for this shape of block: it would be impossible to persuade the cane strands to bend laterally sideways into right angles in the pattern to conform to the block's shape. Such a block will have the holes in each of its sides spaced the same distance as the holes in the corresponding rails of the frame.

The block will have to be suspended centrally as described for the previous two methods, but thereafter the method is different. It can best be described as the normal six-way standard, but with the centre of the pattern cut away to accommodate the block. The vertical strands are laid at either side of the block from top to bottom, but only to the block edge itself when the centre is reached. The middle section of verticals are woven from the top rail into the holes in the top of the block, and into the bottom of it from the bottom rail, in shorter lengths than those which are woven direct from top to bottom. It is the same with the horizontals: these are woven from side to side above and below the block, but the strands of the middle section are woven as far as the block and then back to the side rail. Similarly, the diagonals are woven across from rail to rail until they are interrupted by the block when short diagonals have to be woven into the block and back to the frame. Although the diagonals are in a sense cut into by the block, each must nevertheless be kept in line with its continuation length as if it is one strand.

Beading can be added in any of the ways described in the section on Pegging and Beading (*see* page 83).

The finished back, woven with concentric circles.

RISING SUN

This design gets its name from the fact that the effect of the weaving is to produce a design emulating the rays of the rising sun. It is created by the positioning of a semicircular block of wood, often carved on the front, in the middle of the bottom of the frame, or occasionally at the top. Arms of bergère chairs and settees sometimes have a rising sun effect from a smaller block fixed in one of the corners. Wherever the block may be, the method is virtually the same as that for the Spider's Web.

For all practical purposes, the block can be regarded as the front rail of a normal seat frame; the sections on either side of it correspond to the side rails, and the other rails together correspond to the back rail. It will therefore be apparent that the number of holes in the block is roughly the same as all those in the top and side rails together. Because

the holes in the block will consequently be much smaller in diameter than those in the rest of the frame, the finer sizes of cane are likely to be required for the weaving.

Step 1 is worked from the middle hole of the block to the middle hole in the top of the frame (or bottom, depending whether the block is fixed to the bottom or top). When the block is in the corner of the frame, the strand is taken from the middle hole of the block to the middle hole of all those in the four rails – which is not necessarily the diagonally opposite corner hole.

The strands of *Step 1* radiate from every hole in the block to holes in the outer parts of the frame. The outer frame holes will have been placed so that for the most part the strands of this step will radiate equally from the block. It is only in the parts of the frame nearest to the block that some holes may have to be missed in order

The right arm panel – Step 1 completed.

Steps 1 and 3 completed.

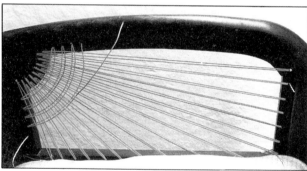

The start of Steps 2 and 4.

to maintain the symmetry of the radiating strands.

Step 3 is then woven to the side of *Step 1.* As the back of the chair is visible, it is vital to thread the strands of *Step 3* through the holes in both frame and block – so that they lie between the holes not already woven by *Step 1* – to give a neat effect.

Steps 2 and *4* are worked together. The first strand of *Step 2* is pegged into the hole in the frame which is next to the block and to the right of it, the strand of *Step 4* being pegged into the corresponding hole on the left of the block. Weave under and over each strand of *Steps 1* and *3*, first with the right-hand strand and then with the other – not too tightly: the diagonal strands will need space to weave into the block between them at a later stage.

When this first row of weaving is completed, each strand goes through its partner's hole on the other side of the block, out to the back of the frame and into the next hole. Weave back in each direction, taking care that the separate rows of weaving alternate. This sequence of weaving with the strands of *Steps 2* and *4* continues until there are no more holes in the block left for the strands to go through. Ensure the arcs formed by each pair of strands aren't too tightly woven, and correspond to the curve of the block; if necessary, using the two bottom corner holes.

At the top of the frame there will be corners which need short strands woven in to fill the frame. These short strands are pegged into suitable holes so as to follow as far as possible the preceding strands of *Steps 2* and *4*.

The diagonals of *Steps 5* and *6* should present no problems. They are woven as in an ordinary seat – over and under the verticals and horizontals. Start the first diagonal from the last hole in the right of the block and weave in a clockwise direction. Most of the doubles will fall on the right of the frame, and most of the misses on the left. With *Step 6,* the corresponding doubles and misses will occur on the opposite sides of the frame to those of *Step 5.* Pull each weaving of the diagonals as taut as possible.

After *Step 5* has been woven, you may find it necessary to tighten up the strands of *Steps 2* and *4,* since the diagonals will have pulled them into their permanent position in the pattern.

Usually no beading is added to this pattern, as the holes in the block are too close together – and the frame holes too far apart – to create a pleasing effect. Every hole is therefore pegged. Pegs for the holes in the block have to be extremely thin yet firm, and you will find that matchsticks fulfil the purpose admirably.

One occasionally comes across chair backs with the Rising Sun pattern in which all the holes, including those in the block, are 'blind' holes. This makes for a quicker job, in that after the first diagonal has been woven it is easier to tighten the strands of *Steps 2* and *4.* However, when cutting those strands to length,

Steps 2 and 4 completed; Step 5 started.

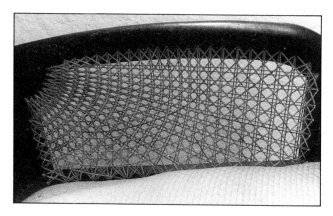

The finished arm.

allowance must be made for the fact that they will be tensioned by hand after the first diagonal is in place, and could be pulled out of their holes. On the other hand, do not be tempted to work a chair back which calls for long strands being woven through every hole, as if it is one with blind holes. Not only would that be cheating, but in any case blind hole caning is never quite as strong as the traditional long-strand method.

CLOSE CANING

Close caning is appropriately named, as the chief feature of the finished work is the fact that every vertical and horizontal strand of cane is interwoven close against its neighbour. The technique is more akin to textile weaving on a loom than it is to 'open' canework. A wide variety of patterns can be achieved using the larger sizes of cane – sometimes No. 4, usually No. 6, even glossy wrapping cane of ³⁄₁₆in (5mm) or wider. There is a particular enchantment in a closely caned seat or panel, especially when light falling on it from different angles emphasizes particular direction of the weave to make it appear an entirely different pattern.

It must be said that this is a time-consuming technique, though amply rewarding. If you can practise on a square or rectangular seat, so much the better: shaped seats (where the front rail is longer than the back) should not be attempted until you have had experience on a simple seat (i.e. involving only right angles). Incidentally, it is invariably seats which are close caned; I have never come across a back or side panel which has been woven in this way, though there is no reason why this should not be done provided they are suitable for the purpose.

The front and side rails of a chair to be close caned must be fractionally lower than the two front posts of the chair legs; and although there are usually frame holes in the rails, these are much more widely spaced than in open cane weaving – eight holes in each rail is not uncommon, and rarely more than a dozen.

To begin with, the frame must have a liner positioned and secured round the inner edge of the seat frame. This is made in one complete length of a large diameter centre cane (anything between No. 13 and No. 15), or palembang cane or a willow wand. Fix this to the inside of the frame with panel pins, but do not drive these home hard. Leave a gap between the liner and the frame to allow the weaving cane to go between.

The liner in place, fixed to the inner edges of the frame with panel pins.

Alternatively, the liner can be tied to the frame with strong fine string at two points close to the corners at the ends of each rail. This string can be removed as the work reaches it. The two ends of the liner should meet in the middle of the back rail with a diagonal cut. When it is brought to the corners, the liner is bent to fit as snugly as possible into them. Make the cane wet at these corners to facilitate bending; a pair of round-nosed pliers is useful in making a tight bend and lessens the chance of the cane splitting. The rest of the cane liner should remain dry.

The holes in the rails are for what is called base caning, to give a firm support to the close canework which will be woven on top of it. Using as large a size of cane as the hole will permit, weave a base consisting of the first four steps of the basic six-way standard pattern. Peg each hole and tap the pegs down into the holes so that they do not protrude above the surface of the rails, since to do so would create a bump in the caning which will be woven over it and cause wear at that point.

Because of the comparative rigidity of the weaving cane, a tension stick should be placed across the seat resting on the side rails, to allow sufficient slack in the warp which is laid over it. This tension stick can be fashioned from a length of dowelling of about ⅝in to ¾in (16mm–19mm) in diameter. There are no rigid rules regarding diameter: the larger the seat area, the greater the diameter. The diameter is also governed by whether you prefer your warp to be tight or loose.

The designs illustrated have mostly been drawn for a three-strand weave, but each can easily be adapted for four- or five-strand patterns. Virtually any loom-weaving regular pattern utilizing the counted thread method is suitable for close caning.

Cut the warp cane into lengths (the strands are laid from front to back across the frame). They must be long enough to extend from the front edge of the front rail to the back edge of the back one, and to go under both rails, with an extra 4in (102mm) allowed at each end. You will need a considerable number of these lengths; when the warp has been fully laid, they will be lying side by side against each other over both front and back rails, so that the rails are completely covered by them (*see* Patterns, page 146).

If there is a decorative weave along the top of each rail, this is put in while the warp is being laid and during the weaving process. It usually consists of three strands. Always keep every strand really damp as you work.

To make the warp, first mark the middle of the front and back rails and the length of the back rail on the front rail. Take a strand which you have already cut to length and lay it from front to back over the tension stick, resting about midway along the side

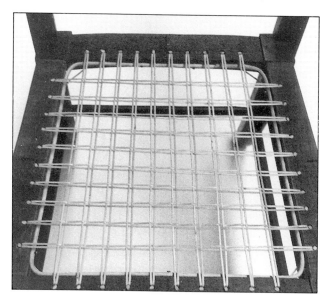

Base caning is laid as for the first four steps of the six-way standard method.

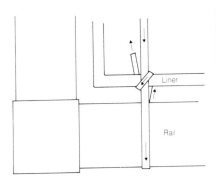

The warp cane is brought over the rail and then under it, up in the centre, over itself and between the liner and the rail.

rails. Then take the front end of the strand underneath the front rail, up on the inside of the frame, loop it over itself, and thread it down between the frame and the liner, pulling the end tight to hold it

securely in place while you do the same thing with the other end of the strand over the back rail: over the tension stick, round and under the back rail, up inside the frame to loop over itself and go down between the frame and the liner, where it also is pulled taut.

That is the way to make the warp, each vertical strand being knotted individually over itself and between the frame and the liner at both ends. The ends of the knots should all point in the same direction. Complete one half of the seat before starting the other. Keep each knot close up against the previous one, and make sure you do not push the middle strand (the one you laid first) over

The warp is laid over the tension stick and kept clear of the base caning. The ends of each strand are knotted into position. For this chair no decoration was added along the rails. Note the space between the last warp strand which has been laid on the left, and the front left corner. This space will in due course have to be filled with shorter warp strands woven into the weft.

The ends of each strand are clamped between the liner and the frame against the next strand.

the middle marks on the front and back rails.

While you are laying the warp – and also while you will be weaving the horizontal pattern – you will need to cover the base strands with the warp and weft ones. Include the base strands beneath the warp strands and incorporate them into the loops you make prior to knotting.

It is more than likely that the bend of the liner in the corners will prevent you from knotting the last warp strands neatly and securely, in which case you can fill the extra spaces at each end of the back and front rails by wrapping the last strand once or twice round the rails and the liner, tucking the end firmly away between frame and liner.

To weave the decorative strands along the front rail, cut as many as are required for the pattern, each fractionally shorter than the length of

the rail. Work out where the central part of the decoration is and place the appropriate number of strands (depending on the pattern) under the initial middle warp strand on the front rail. As you place the remaining warp strands in position, the decorative strands are laid under or over them as the pattern may require before the warp strands are knotted. The warp will hold these decorative strands in place. The same procedure is followed for the decoration along the back rail, and also along the side rails during the weaving process.

For a shaped seat – one with the front rail longer than the back, no matter whether it is shaped or straight – the warping will need to be done differently as it approaches the side rails. Once you have wrapped the full length of the back rail with warp strands and the equivalent distance on the front rail up to the marks, there will inevitably be an uncovered space at each end of the front rail. If there is room at each end for not more than four strands, it is acceptable to wrap a strand four times round the bare section of front rail and liner. The ends of these lengths of wrapping are then tucked away securely between the frame and the undersides of the wrapping strands for 3in or 4in (76mm–102mm). Some people secure them with a small tack to remove any chance of their slipping out, but that should not be necessary if the strand is tucked away properly; as it dries out, it will become difficult to remove.

Wrapping the bare front rail ends with more than four wraps would leave an unacceptable gap in the pattern at these two points. When the space is greater than could be covered by a four-wrap thickness, the warp has to be made to reach as close as possible to the side rails. So carry on knotting-in the warp strands along the front rail, wrapping the last strand around rail and liner for a couple of turns and securing it by tucking in. However, do not try to loop and knot the ends of these warp strands on to the back liner. Leave them loose,

knotted at the front, to be positioned after the weaving has been completed.

The simplest weaving pattern consists of double strands woven alternately over and under adjacent warp strands. Because of the comparative inflexibility of the cane, there are bound to be gaps on the side rails between each row of weaving; these gaps will be covered as you weave. The decorative edges along the side rails will also be woven in as the work proceeds, in the same way as they were for the laying of the warp over the front and back rails.

For the weaving, it is not necessary to cut the weaving strands to length if

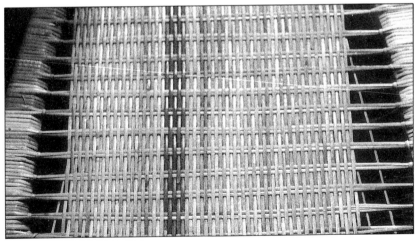

A simple pattern. In this variation the pairs of weft strands are separated from each other by several wraps. For this pattern it is not necessary to cut each weft strand to length or to knot it into the liner, but long strands can be used. Note that the horizontal base strands have been incorporated beneath the pairs of weft strands. Note also that it is advisable to select your strands carefully: a block of darker warp strands left of centre in this picture does little to enhance the appearance.

you are to use this simple pattern. The longest available strands of cane will be required. Take one end of the weaver and knot it on to the liner at the corner of the front rail on the left; you may have to ease a way for it through the warp strands. The other end is brought out to the side from under the side rail, up the outside, over the top, down the inside of the frame and liner, and round and over again, thus making a wrap. It is now ready to begin the weave. You may like to use a long weaving needle to raise the warp strands before inserting the end of the weaving strand; any long thin piece of metal will do, but fingers are best! Weave under one warp strand, over the next, under and over alternately across to the opposite rail. The cane is then wrapped round the rail against the corner. Keep each strand close against the previous one on the side rails as you work, and straight and parallel across the seat.

Having brought the first weaving strand across and wrapped it once round the side rail, bring the end up inside the frame and loop it over itself before taking it back down and under the rail and over the top. It is then fed through the loop before being woven back across the warp in the same sequence, so that it lies against the first weaving strand. Take it over the left side rail, under this, up on the inside, and loop it over both weaving strands. Make another wrap and weave it across to the other rail – this time over the first warp and under the next, thus reversing the weaving sequence. Make a wrap round the right rail; loop the strand over itself; bring it out under the frame and round over the top so that it can go through the loop again, and weave across to the left rail. This sequence continues until you reach the back of the frame. You can remove the tension stick after you have completed about one-third of the weaving.

To finish off, tuck the end of the weaving strand between the side wraps and the frame for 2in or 3in (51mm–76mm), and pull tight. Tack the end of the strand to the inside of the frame if you prefer.

During the weaving, be careful not to catch any of the base caning into the work. No damage is caused if this occurs, but it is something a good cane weaver would never do. Remember also to incorporate the base canes into the loops at the side rails, as you did with the knotting of the warps at the front and back rails.

Joins should be made by knotting the end of the old strand round the liner and knotting the new strand next to it.

For more complex patterns such as those illustrated here, no wraps are required round the side rails. Each weaving strand is knotted individually on to the liner along the sides, exactly in the manner as for the warp. Follow the pattern carefully, counting the warp strands with each weave. The tension stick can be removed as soon as you feel that the weft is taking up the tension on the warp. Do not leave its removal until you are too far into the work, or you may find the earlier weaving strands will be made loose and have to be re-knotted.

Keep the strands straight and parallel, and push the knots tightly against each other as you proceed. It cannot be too firmly stressed that the strands must always be kept thoroughly damp, particularly at the ends where the knots have to be made.

When you reach the back of the seat there may be space on each of the side rails which, because of the corner bends of the liner, the weaver cannot be knotted to satisfactorily. To end the weaving, cover this spare space with wraps round the rail and liner before tucking the end of the strand between the knots and the frame, weaving it under and over three strands at a time for a distance of 3in (76mm) or so before pulling tight.

If, when you are nearing the completion of the weaving, you discover that the warp strands are either too tight or too loose, dampen the warp knots at the back of the frame and either loosen or tighten them as the case may be before continuing with the weaving.

In both these weaving methods on a seat where the front rail is wider than the back, it will still be necessary

In this pattern (which includes a simple rail decoration) every strand of both warp and weft is knotted into the liner at each end. Shorter warp strands have been knotted at each end of the front rail and woven into the weft for as far towards the back as they will comfortably go.

to attend to the spare warp strands which were knotted on to the liner at each end of the front rail. Making sure that all the warp and weft strands in these areas are thoroughly dampened, weave each warp strand firmly into the pattern, one side of the frame at a time, starting with the strand which lies next to the last completely laid warp strand, and weaving it as far back into the weft as it will comfortably go without distorting the pattern. Work it back along the same weave underneath and against itself. Take the adjacent loose warp strand, weave it similarly into the pattern for as far as it will go, and weave that end back in the same way. Do the same with each of these loose warp strands on each side.

With a curved front rail, individual lengths of cane can be woven horizontally into the pattern to fill in the unpatterned area between the frame and the first row of weaving. Weave the ends of these short weavers back under themselves as you did with the side warp strands.

Turn the chair over so that you can work on the underside of the seat. Pull the end of every knotted strand away from the bottom of the seat, thus clamping the ends between the adjacent strands. Cut off these knot ends to leave about ¼in (6mm) of cane – long enough for the knots not to slip. Do this with every knotted strand. Then trim off the short warp

and weft strands to about 1in (13mm); the compactness of the weaving will hold them in place.

Having to knot both ends of upwards of perhaps 200 strands of cane is a laborious way of passing the time! You may think it boring to lay the warp in this way; but I do assure you that once you have got into the weaving and can see the pattern unfolding, you will not want to stop until the job is done. Because the work is so labour-intensive, chairs with close-caned patterned seats are not seen in furnishing shops nowadays. Pre-woven cane panels in the basic weave of over one, under one can be purchased, but they cannot be affixed to an old chair which was specifically designed for close canework to be woven by hand.

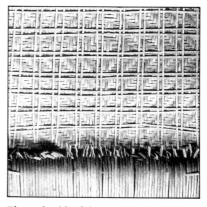

The underside of the seat showing the base caning still virtually separated from the woven seat and the knotted ends waiting to be pulled tight and cut off. The ends of extra strands have been woven in on the underside of the work.

BINDER CANE

The widest of seating cane, from ³/₁₆in–¹/₄in (5mm–6mm) in width – known as binder or glossy wrapping cane – can be used to weave a number of simple patterns and can be worked in two ways. For this type of seat you will require a supply of small (no longer than ¹/₂in or 13mm) gimp pins, a small hammer, sharp knife or shears or sturdy scissors, and a pair of long-nosed pliers. A long weaving needle may also be useful.

This cane can be used on any seat frame, with or without corner posts; but since the latter, in my experience, are not only uncommon but more than difficult to work, I shall describe the two methods suitable for frames with posts. The only requirement is that the inner sides of the rails must be reasonably flat.

Binder cane is thick and for our purposes requires soaking for 30 minutes or more in hot water at a temperature which remains reasonably constant at about 140°F (60°C) until it is really supple. It must be kept supple throughout the work.

Mark the middle of both front and back rails. If the corner posts are round, pin one or two short strands to the top of the side rail, wrap them round the front rail at the corner and pin them to the inside of that rail. Do this on all corners if necessary before the weaving starts. This is to cover any bare wood at the ends of the rails which otherwise would be exposed.

Incidentally, when pinning the ends of strands into place do not pin into them at the very end or they will split.

Pin a length of cane to the inside of the front rail a short way from the left corner so that the weaving end hangs down. Bring it under the front rail and round it to lie against the corner or against any short strands you may have laid. Then take it over to the back rail, round it and underneath, and pin it to the inside of the rail, where it is cut off. A second long strand is pinned next to the first on the inside of the front rail; bring this strand also under the front rail, over against the first and across to the back rail.

Wraps will be needed between pairs of strands along the front and back rails, but to maintain regularity more wraps will need to be laid over the front rail than the back, because of course the front rail is longer than the back. You will have to use your judgement in this matter, for though it is usual in this pattern to wrap twice round the back rail between each pair of warp strands, the number of wraps on the front rail is governed by the extra distance between the warps. There may be two, three or even four short wraps between the front warp pairs in order to keep them equally spaced. You should organize these wraps so that the strand against the middle marks lines up with both the front and back marks. On the other half of the frame you will copy the number of short wraps between the warp strands on the first half so that the two halves become as it were miror images of each other.

So, wrap the last strand (which is the second of the first pair of strands) round the back rail twice before pinning it to the inside of the back rail and cutting off the end.

The next strand is pinned to the inside of the front rail next to the previous strand. This one is wrapped round the front rail for as many times as you have decided is required, before being taken across to the back rail and pinned on the inside again. Pin a fourth strand at the front, take it over to the back rail, wrap round it twice, pin it to the inside of the back rail, and cut off.

Continue pinning and wrapping in this way until you get to the middle of the back and front rails. Hopefully the same strand will reach both marks at the same time, either as a warp – if there is to be an odd number of warps – or as a wrap – for an even number. If your judgement has been faulty

over the number of wraps between warps, simply undo the last pair of warp strands and add another wrap to the last set. Then continue laying the warp over the frame to the opposite side.

Remember to keep these thick strands of cane thoroughly damp at all times during the work. This is particularly necessary on a frame which has a shallow curve on the front rail. If the strands are allowed to dry out while they are being worked, they will not shape themselves to the contours of the rail but instead will tend to lie flat with their edges nearest the corner slightly proud, thus encouraging them to slip over the edge of the previous strand.

For the same reason – to reduce the possibility of slipping – the weft is

The completed warp. Note that there is only a single strand at the right-hand edge – an extra one can be woven in to improve the appearance when the weft is completed, though it will be a purely cosmetic job and not wrapped round the rails or fixed to the frame in any way.

started from the back of the side rails, where the distance across the frame is narrower than at the front, the side rails thereby slanting towards the back.

Pin a strand on top of the left rail against the corner, short end pointing outwards. Bring the strand down on the inside of the rail, round it, up on the outside, and over the top to lie on top of itself and covering the pinhead. Start weaving over and under each alternate pair of warp strands. Keep the strand straight. When it reaches the right side rail, take it down the outside and up on the inside, and pin it on the top of the rail next to itself.

Pin a second strand against the edge of the first one and weave the same over and under sequence so that it lies next to the first strand across to the opposite rail. Lay it over the pinned end of the previous strand, then round under the rail to be pinned against itself. Every weft strand will lie over its own end on the left rail and over the previous end on the right rail.

All pairs of strands are pinned and woven in this way. The weaving of

The finished seat, with the additional single warp and weft strands against the front and left rails woven in.

alternate strand pairs, however, is opposite to the previous pair: under where they went over, over where they went under. The final weft strand has to be pinned to the inside of the right rail because the top of the rail will already be covered with strands.

As a last security measure, four lengths of the largest available size of centre cane (certainly not less than size No. 14) should be tacked to the inside of the rail. This is not absolutely necessary, but it does hide the pinheads and holds the strands in place should their ends split and come away from the pins. Two lengths of centre cane will suffice, because each piece is split down the middle. The flat edge is pinned at various points along the inside of each rail, between strands rather than through them.

The second method is to work with long continuous strands. As you will see from the chair illustrated on this page, this pattern can be achieved on frames with quite pronounced rail curves.

This is a comparatively simple method, in that you do not have to cut each warp and weft strand, though because of the curves I did pin them into place to prevent them from slipping sideways as I worked.

Start by laying the warp from the left corner of the back rail. Pin the end of a long strand to the top of the rail and bring it under and over the top so that it lies over the pin. It is then brought forward to the left corner of the front rail, round underneath and up on the inside. You will notice from the illustration that the back rail is considerably shorter

The warp is being laid over a seat frame with pronounced curved rails. Although it is not always possible to do, the pattern for this particular seat allows joins to be made by knotting the new end with the old by a reef knot, as can be seen. Of course, such joins must be made on the underside of the seat.

than the front. Therefore there is only one wrap, occasionally two, between the warp strands on the back rail to keep them roughly equidistant, whereas on the front rail there are mostly three with two between the warp pairs at the middle.

Keep the strand with which you are working thoroughly damp – though not saturated – so that it moulds itself to the curve as it goes over the rails and hugs them tight, making contact everywhere on the underside (non-glossy side). To persuade them to stay in place, every alternate short wrap and each individual warp strand is pinned to the underside of front and back rails. This pinning sequence also applies to the weft strands.

Make short wraps round the front rail against the first warp strand – as many wraps as you judge to be needed – then take it under the rail and under the frame to the back rail. Wrap as many times as necessary round the back rail, then bring it up the outside of the rail and over to the front. Make short wraps, take it back underneath, make wraps, then bring it back over the top to the front rail again. Continue laying the warp in this way with single strands across to the right side rail, each half balancing the other in the spacing and number of wraps. The warp will finish at the front right corner, where the strand is pinned to the underside of the front

rail and a few inches are left hanging. Carefully fold this loose end sideways and weave between alternate strands on the underside of the front rail for a few weaves before pulling tight and cutting off. The weaving of this pattern is under three, over three, but staggered with each weft strand. There will be no short wraps between the weft strands.

Pin a new long strand to the top of the left rail at the back against the corner. Bring it down on the inside, round under the rail and over itself on the top to cover the pin, then using the long steel needle weave under three and over three warp strands across to the right side rail. Take the strand round the right rail and weave the strands beneath the seat similarly – under three and over three alternately across to the left rail. Bring it up and over the left rail, and weave first under two strands, then over three and under three across to the right rail. Take it round the rail again to weave back under the seat, first under two, then over three and under three to the left rail. Round this rail again, and weave under one, then over three and under three across to the right. Weave back underneath – under one, over three and under three back to the left. This completes the first half of the simple pattern.

The second half begins with Row 4 and goes over three warp strands and under three across the seat and back

in the same sequence underneath.
Row 5 – over two, then under three
and over three etc. Row 6 – over one,
under three, over three etc. This
completes the pattern.

Row 7 begins the pattern again –
under three, over three across the
seat, above and then beneath the
frame; and so you continue with
these six staggered rows to the front
of the seat, pinning the strands on the
underside of the frame as you
progress. It does not matter if the
numbers of warp and weft strands are
not multiples of three, as the pattern
will work itself out. Finish by pinning
the end of the last weft strand to the
inside of the rail and working a few
inches of it back into the weave,
following the same course but below

the existing strand so that it will not
show on the top of the seat.

Finally, pin four strips of split
centre cane over the pins on the
underside of the rails, as in the
previous method.

New lengths of strand are added by
first pinning the old end to the
underside, leaving 1in or 2in
(26mm–51mm) lying against the rail
which will be covered by later
strands. The new strand is pinned to
the top of the rail, brought round to
lie over itself as with the starting
strands of the warp and weft.

Decorative strips of binder cane can
be added on the top of all four side
rails in both these methods, as
described in the section on Close
Caning on page 123.

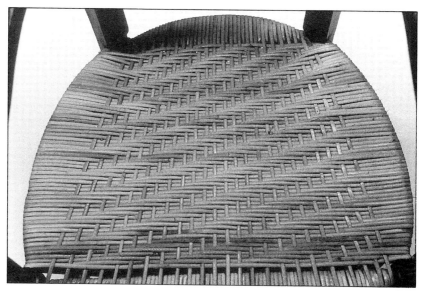

The finished seat.

PRE-WOVEN CANE

Pre-woven cane, sometimes known as machine cane or cane webbing, is ordinary seating cane partially woven mechanically on looms, only the diagonals being woven by hand. There is a variety of patterns in both open and close cane, the most common being the six-way standard, available from suppliers in any length up to 50ft (15.2m) and in widths of between 12in and 36in (30.5cm and 91.4cm); it is usually sold by the square foot (30.5cm × 30.5cm). If you have such a seat to be renewed, it is advisable to show your supplier a piece of the old seat so that the size of the pattern can be matched (the measurement between the repeats of the pattern in the six-way standard does vary). You will also need a length of 'spline' or centre cane of the appropriate diameter.

Replacing a pre-woven cane seat or panel is easier than it looks. If you are thinking of converting a traditional hand-woven frame with holes drilled through it into one which will take a pre-woven cane panel, a considerable amount of preparatory work will need to be carried out first, however, with a router or a drill. Since not every traditionally-woven frame is suitable for such a conversion (the thickness of the frame is of no little importance) I do not propose to describe how to do it. Pre-woven cane is quite commonplace nowadays, but it is not a twentieth-century invention. In fact a loom was set up to produce it commercially during the last century in America. But my attitude is that if a chairmaker had wished his seat to be pre-woven, he would have made it possible for that to be done. I prefer to return a seat to its original state; who am I to say that the designer of the piece of furniture was wrong?

Pre-woven cane panels are not installed exclusively in seats, of course. Coffee tables, bedheads, screens, room dividers – in the earlier days of motoring, the side panels of some vehicles – all use the material; the larger the area to be caned, the more useful is pre-woven cane. However, for this book we shall concentrate on the renewal of seats which were originally designed to take pre-woven cane.

The only tools you will need are a light hammer, an old screwdriver, a sharp knife and a few wooden wedges. The legs of a few spring-loaded clothes pegs can be used as wedges: remove the spring, and you have two already made. The screwdriver should be slightly narrower than the width of the groove in which the cane is seated.

The first job is to remove the old spline and the pre-woven cane. With a sharp blade, cut down each side of the spline into the groove all the way round the frame, to help loosen it. This spline is holding the cane in place. The screwdriver is inserted at the joins and the spline levered gently out, taking care not to splinter the woodwork; in a shaped frame there is usually only one join, in the middle of the back, and at the corners in a straight-edged frame. It is preferable to lever from the inside edge of the groove, as any damage caused to the woodwork will be largely concealed by the new panel. Put a length of the old spline to one side as it can be used as additional wedges.

If the spline proves difficult to remove, it is probably because there is wood glue holding it firm. In this case, apply warm water to soften it up, letting it soak in before trying again to remove the spline.

With the spline removed, the next operation is to remove every particle of old cane from the groove. Cut it away all around the inside of the frame, then start to remove it from the groove. Soften the glue which is holding the cane down in the groove, then use the screwdriver to scrape it out. The groove must be perfectly smooth, bottom as well as sides, before the new panel can be inserted. Careful sand-papering when the wood is dry is recommended as the final preparation, particularly the top inside edge of the groove so as to remove any possible sharpness of the wood which could rub against the new cane and cause it to break.

To assess the amount of pre-woven cane needed, measure from the outer edges of the grooves from side to side, and from front to back, and add at least 3in (76mm) to each measurement. This is to allow for the depth of the groove and for sufficient cane round the edges for you to hold and pull taut. The diameter of the centre cane spline should be $1/16$in (1.5mm) less than the width of the groove at the surface.

Soak the new pre-woven panel, cut to size, in reasonably hot water (50°C or 120°F) for about a couple of hours so that the cane becomes pliable. Drain off the surplus water, but do not let the panel dry out. As you put it into place you will be stretching it; as it dries in position it will tighten up, creating a firm seat.

Centre the panel on the seat frame so that the horizontals and verticals are properly lined up with the grooves, the pattern is not askew, and there is an equal amount of spare cane lying beyond the groove on all four sides.

Take one wedge and with the hammer tap it gently down on the cane in the middle of the back rail so that the cane at that point is seated firmly on the bottom of the groove.

You will find that as the wedge is being tapped in at the back, the front edge of the cane panel will be pulled slightly inwards. Make sure that the front edge remains parallel. Leave that wedge in place, holding the panel down in the groove, and take another one to tap down the cane for about 1in (25mm) on either side of it. Remove the wedges; tap in a short length of the old spline which you have kept, to hold the cane temporarily in position in the middle of the back rail while you transfer your attention to the front rail.

Pull the cane taut towards you, and with a wedge tap it into the groove in the middle of the front rail. Check that the pattern is not getting out of alignment. Tap another wedge to seat the cane into the groove for 1in (25mm) or so on either side of the central wedge, just as you did at the back, then replace them with a short length of the old spline.

Before repeating the process on the side rails, carefully remove the cotton selvedge on one edge of the panel first; this was woven in during the manufacture to stop it unravelling. Then pull out all the vertical and horizontal strands of cane that are lying over and outside the groove. Having removed these, pull out the diagonal strands which are also lying over and outside the groove. The removal of these strands facilitates the tapping of the cane into the

bottom of the groove at the corners by reducing the tension of the cane as it is being tapped into place.

Using the wedges again, tap the cane into the middle of one of the side rails as before, and insert a length of old spline to hold it there. Pull the panel taut on the opposite rail, ensuring that the pattern is still centralized, and tap it into the groove to be held with another short length of spline. The panel should now be anchored firmly at four points in the middle of each rail. With a wedge, tap in the remainder of the cane at the back towards one corner, and hold it there with a piece of spline. Do the same on the opposite rail at the front, first pulling the panel taut but not out of shape. Then tap the rest of the cane into the back groove, holding it with a piece of spline, and do likewise at the front.

Now move to a side rail and tap half of the rest of the cane into the groove; then to the opposite rail; then back to the other one, and so on until the panel is secure in the groove on both sides as well as back and front, and in the corners. All the while you are tapping the panel into place, keep checking to see that the pattern remains central and taut. As it dries and shrinks, any misalignment will be accentuated.

Unless the centre cane you are using for the new spline is exceptionally dry, it should not be soaked. If you do need to moisten it, merely dip it into warm water for a few moments. A soaked spline of centre cane will split as it is tapped over the cane in the groove.

Remove the temporary old spline wedges and lay a generous amount of wood glue into the groove over the cane before inserting the new spline. If your seat has rounded corners, the new spline can be inserted in one continuous length. Starting at the middle of the back, using the hammer and one of the clothes peg legs laid on its side (to spread the weight of the hammer and prevent indentations in the spline), carefully tap the spline down into place to hold the cane firmly, until the crown is level with the woodwork of the frame. When the whole length of spline has been inserted, make a butt joint at the back.

For a square-cornered seat, four pieces of spline are cut to length and tapped in by the same method. Mitre joints are preferable at the corners.

When the spline is being tapped home, it is likely that some wood glue will ooze out of the groove. This should be wiped off before it sets, but not before the excess pre-woven cane has been cut away. Using a sharp knife held at about 60°, cut away the excess just below the outer edge of the groove. Wipe the frame clean, leave the cane to dry, and the job is done.

If the groove is exceptionally deep, it may be necessary to shape a large length of centre cane for the spline into an oval with flattened sides. If

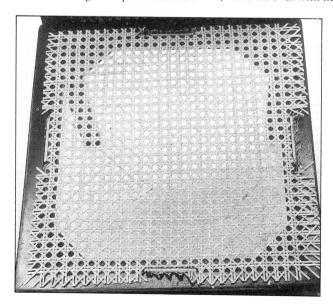

The panel has been pulled taut laterally before the two temporary pieces of spline are inserted in the side grooves.

this is not possible, two lengths of spline can be inserted, one above the other, with a layer of wood glue in between. What is important is that the spline should seat firmly on the cane at the bottom of the groove, and that the crown of it should be level with the woodwork of the frame. Compacted into the groove, it holds the cane in place.

The finished seat.

PATCHING

You may feel depressed by the prospect of having to completely re-weave a panel even though the hole is small – no more than a few broken strands needing to be replaced, not the whole lot. You do not need to re-weave it all – the hole can be patched! Although patching is not recommended on a seat, it is quite acceptable for a back or side panel which takes relatively little pressure.

Individual lengths of cane should be prepared – of the same size as the broken ones, and 4in (102mm) longer than the strand to be replaced. These separate lengths have to be woven accurately into the existing pattern. Replacement strands should ideally be carefully withdrawn from a discarded seat or a panel which has been cut away from another chair, since by using good lengths of old cane which are of about the same colour, the patch will not be as noticeable as if new cane is used.

Extreme care is needed for the work, which begins with the damaged area as well as the replacement strands being thoroughly dampened so that they are flexible. But even when damp, the adjacent strands of the good part of the panel can still be brittle enough to break. So be *very careful*; do not hurry the job.

Taking one replacement strand at a time, start weaving, following the under and over sequence as may be appropriate. Verticals, horizontals and diagonals each have their own sequence, which can be easily followed by studying the undamaged parts of the pattern as you are weaving. Begin 2in (51mm) from the break. The replacement strand must lie on top of the broken one, to finish 2in (51mm) beyond the break. The overlap at each end is sufficient for the cane to be held in place without recourse to any adhesive. When finally in place, each end must be carefully trimmed so that the join can neither be seen nor felt.

Where strands have broken at the very edge of the pattern close to the beading, you may have to loosen the beading for a few inches at either side of the hole or holes in which the damaged canes lie. This loosening of the beading (which also needs to be

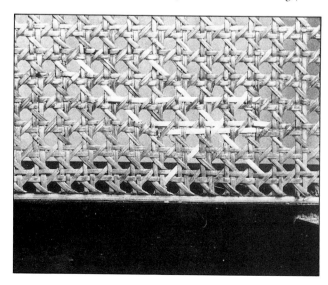

Patching should not be attempted for large areas of broken canework, nor for seats or where there is heavy pressure on the work.

dampened) will not be necessary if the replacement strand has to go down into a hole containing the couching cane. Simply ease the beading and couching canes away sufficiently to allow enough room for the end of the replacement cane to be inserted. Then lightly tap the couching cane back into position.

However, if the replacement strand has to be inserted into a pegged hole, the beading cane must be loosened. First cut away the section of the couching cane holding the beading which covers the pegged hole; this allows access to the peg which can either be tapped out, or a small hole can be drilled into the peg itself, sufficiently large to receive the end of the replacement strand. A dab of adhesive on the end before inserting it helps to hold it in place.

To replace the beading, thoroughly dampen the underside of all the cane (loops as well as couching) at the points where the couching cane has been cut out so that the original ends can be knotted in with the new length of couching cane which you are about to install. With the new couching cane, re-sew the beading into place and knot both ends of the couching canes on the other side of the frame.

If you have no old strands of cane to use as replacements, then of course new cane can be used, but the patching will show up unless you colour-match each separate strand, back and front. The older and more brittle the original cane, the greater the need to patch with old rather than new strands. Like the biblical reference to putting new wine into old bottles, so also does new cane against old tend to cause the latter to deteriorate sooner than it would otherwise do.

CARE OF SEATING CANE

The glossy appearance of seating cane comes from its naturally silicious surface. This is what gives a seat its incredible durability and strength, and is also what makes the surface virtually non-porous. In course of time the natural straw colour of the cane darkens from usage, and I personally prefer to leave a new piece of caning looking new – knowing full well that after a few months it will have mellowed to a warm shade of brown.

Of course, there are circumstances where it is necessary to colour-match the new work with the old – e.g. in the case of a bergère chair panel which has been renewed and does not match the colour of the rest of the canework. Water-based stains are of little use because of the non-porosity of the glossy surface. A shellac coating is commonly used but this should be applied with care, as little as possible being allowed to get on to the underside of the work, for if the cane is sealed on both surfaces with any impermeable stain its life is reduced by being made brittle. Even then, the stain can wear off to reveal sections of it which are nearly the original colour.

However, it is worth noting that the makers of rattan furniture in the Far East have turned from their customary use of shellac as a coating system to others which are more durable. Nitro-cellulose coatings are also being displaced by a variety of other types available – acid-catalysed coatings, polyurethane, polyester, and ultra-violet durable coatings are all being used by Far Eastern manufacturers of rattan furniture, choice being dependent upon a number of factors including type of rattan, design of furniture, finished quality and cost.

To preserve a cane seat for as long as possible in its untreated condition, and to prevent undue sagging from constant use, it can be tightened by sponging or spraying with warm water once a month. Plastic spray bottles for indoor plants, cheaply available from any garden centre, are ideal. Spray a fine mist of warm water on to the top and the underside of the seat, and let it dry out naturally. The polished woodwork should of course be protected during this operation, and any water which accidentally comes in contact with it should be wiped off at once. Refrain from trying to speed the drying with a hair dryer or similar household hot air gadget: artificial drying will not let it tighten properly. Neither should you sit on it while it is still damp, otherwise the cane will stretch and you will never get it really tight again.

Finally, try to arrange your furniture so that no piece of woven canework is near a radiator, or gas or open fire. Seating cane comes from a living plant, remember, and does not take kindly either to being sealed in with colouring matter or being subjected to a permanent dried-out condition.

PATTERNS

A selection of patterns based on the three-cord block. Any of these can be used or adapted for cord weaving, many also for close caning and seating in binder cane.

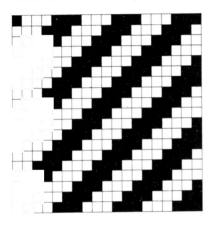

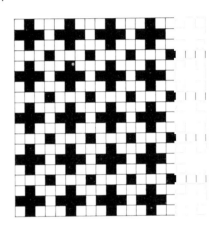

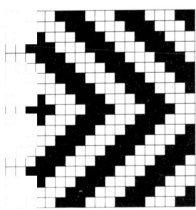

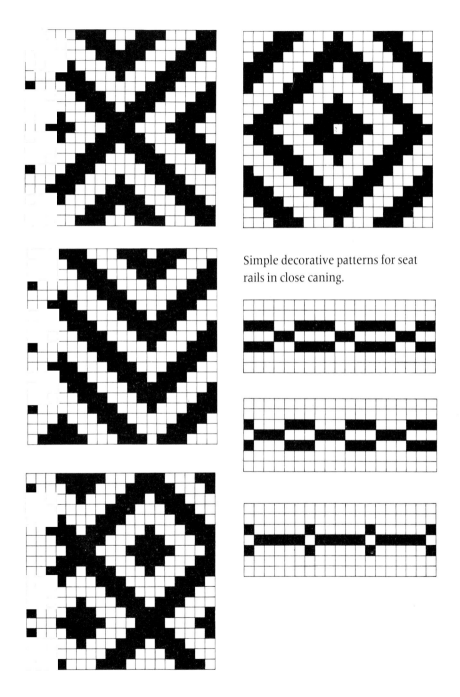

Simple decorative patterns for seat rails in close caning.

SUPPLIERS OF MATERIALS

Fred Aldous Ltd
37 Lever Street, Manchester
M60 1UX
Tel: 061 236 2477

Chair seating cane, centre cane, seagrass

Berrycraft Supplies
Acadia, Swansbrook Lane, Horam,
Heathfield, East Sussex TN21 0LD
Tel: 043 53 2383

*Chair seating cane, fibre rush, seagrass,
Danish cord, pre-woven cane, craft tools
and books*

The Cane Store
207 Blackstock Road, Highbury Vale,
London N5 2LL
Tel: 071 354 4210

*Chair seating cane, fibre rush, Danish
cord, craft tools*

Country Chairmen
Home Farm, Ardington, Nr Wantage,
Oxfordshire OX12 8PY
Tel: 0235 833614

*English freshwater rushes, chair seating
cane, seagrass*

John Excell
The Cane Workshop, The Gospel Hall,
Westport, Langport, Somerset
Tel: 0460 281 636

Chair seating cane, rush, craft tools

The Handicraft Shop
47 Northgate, Canterbury,
Kent CT1 1BE
Tel: 0227 451188

*Chair seating cane, centre cane, Dutch
rush, fibre rush, seagrass, craft tools*

Jacobs, Young & Westbury Ltd
JYW House, Bridge Road, Haywards
Heath, Sussex RH16 1TZ
Tel: 0444 412411

*Dutch rush, fibre rush, seagrass, cord,
chair seating cane, centre cane, craft tools*

Iorwerth Pritchard
17 Heathcote Grove, North
Chingford, London E4 6RZ
Tel: 081 529 2884
*Danish cord. Instructions given in cane
and rush weaving*

Specialist Crafts Ltd
PO Box 247, Leicester LE1 9QS
Tel: 0533 510405
*Chair seating cane, centre cane, seagrass,
cord, rush, craft tools*

Tenterden Craft Centre
Station Road, Tenterden, Kent
TN30 6SG
Tel: 0580 763326
*Chair seating cane, centre cane, pre-
woven cane, Dutch rush, cord, seagrass*

Materials can be purchased from
these suppliers by mail order.

METRIC CONVERSION TABLE

INCHES TO MILLIMETRES AND CENTIMETRES

MM = Millimetres   CM = Centimetres

INCHES	MM	CM	INCHES	CM	INCHES	CM
1/8	3	0.3	9	22.9	30	76.2
1/4	6	0.6	10	25.4	31	78.7
3/8	10	1.0	11	27.9	32	81.3
1/2	13	1.3	12	30.5	33	83.8
5/8	16	1.6	13	33.0	34	86.4
3/4	19	1.9	14	35.6	35	88.9
7/8	22	2.2	15	38.1	36	91.4
1	25	2.5	16	40.6	37	94.0
1 1/4	32	3.2	17	43.2	38	96.5
1 1/2	38	3.8	18	45.7	39	99.1
1 3/4	44	4.4	19	48.3	40	101.6
2	51	5.1	20	50.8	41	104.1
2 1/2	64	6.4	21	53.3	42	106.7
3	76	7.6	22	55.9	43	109.2
3 1/2	89	8.9	23	58.4	44	111.8
4	102	10.2	24	61.0	45	114.3
4 1/2	114	11.4	25	63.5	46	116.8
5	127	12.7	26	66.0	47	119.4
6	152	15.2	27	68.6	48	121.9
7	178	17.8	28	71.1	49	124.5
8	203	20.3	29	73.7	50	127.0

INDEX

TITLES AVAILABLE FROM GMC PUBLICATIONS LTD

BOOKS

Woodworking Plans and Projects	GMC Publications	Making Dolls' House Furniture	Patricia King
40 More Woodworking Plans and Projects	GMC Publications	Making and Modifying Woodworking Tools	Jim Kingshott
Woodworking Crafts Annual	GMC Publications	The Workshop	Jim Kingshott
Woodworkers' Career and Educational Source Book	GMC Publications	Sharpening: The Complete Guide	Jim Kingshott
Woodworkers' Courses & Source Book	GMC Publications	Turning Wooden Toys	Terry Lawrence
Green Woodwork	Mike Abbott	Making Board, Peg and Dice Games	Jeff & Jennie Loader
Making Little Boxes from Wood	John Bennett	The Complete Dolls' House Book	Jean Nisbett
The Incredible Router	Jeremy Broun	Furniture Projects for the Home	Ernest Parrott
Electric Woodwork	Jeremy Broun	Making Money from Woodturning	Ann & Bob Phillips
Woodcarving: A Complete Course	Ron Butterfield	Members' Guide to Marketing	Jack Pigden
Making Fine Furniture: Projects	Tom Darby	Woodcarving Tools and Equipment	Chris Pye
Restoring Rocking Horses	Clive Green & Anthony Dew	Making Tudor Dolls' Houses	Derek Rowbottom
Heraldic Miniature Knights	Peter Greenhill	Making Georgian Dolls' Houses	Derek Rowbottom
Practical Crafts: Seat Weaving	Ricky Holdstock	Making Period Dolls' House Furniture	Derek & Sheila Rowbottom
Multi-centre Woodturning	Ray Hopper	Woodturning: A Foundation Course	Keith Rowley
Complete Woodfinishing	Ian Hosker	Turning Miniatures in Wood	John Sainsbury
Woodturning: A Source Book of Shapes	John Hunnex	Pleasure and Profit from Woodturning	Reg Sherwin
Making Shaker Furniture	Barry Jackson	Making Unusual Miniatures	Graham Spalding
Upholstery: A Complete Course	David James	Woodturning Wizardry	David Springett
Upholstery Techniques and Projects	David James	Furniture Projects	Rod Wales
Designing and Making Wooden Toys	Terry Kelly	Decorative Woodcarving	Jeremy Williams

VIDEOS

Dennis White Teaches Woodturning

Part 1	Turning Between Centres
Part 2	Turning Bowls
Part 3	Boxes, Goblets and Screw Threads
Part 4	Novelties and Projects
Part 5	Classic Profiles
Part 6	Twists and Advanced Turning

Jim Kingshott   Sharpening the Professional Way

Ray Gonzalez   Carving a Figure: The Female Form

GMC Publications regularly produces new books and videos on a wide range of woodworking and craft subjects, and an increasing number of specialist magazines, all available on subscription:

MAGAZINES

WOODCARVING   WOODTURNING   BUSINESSMATTERS

All these publications are available through bookshops and newsagents, or may be ordered by post from the publishers at 166 High Street, Lewes, East Sussex BN7 1XU, telephone (0273) 477374, fax (0273) 478606.

Credit card orders are accepted. Please write or phone for the latest information.